A BOOKLOVER'S GUIDE
TO NEW YORK

Ex Libris

BOOKS FOR EVER

A BOOKLOVER'S GUIDE TO NEW YORK

CLEO LE-TAN

DRAWINGS BY PIERRE LE-TAN

RIZZOLI
NEW YORK

New York · Paris · London · Milan

CONTENTS

PREFACE

People love books. I am one of those people. My siblings and I grew up surrounded by shelves and shelves and piles and piles of books, which occupied at least half of our childhood flat. To call my father an obsessive collector of printed matter would be an understatement.

As a teenager, I spent much of my time hiding in majestic, beautiful, sometimes abandoned libraries in grand old buildings. I puttered around Paris and London, uncovering hidden treasures in weird bookstalls on the banks of the Seine and hunting down dusty antique shops only my dad knew of. The cast of characters I encountered along the way were as fascinating as the literature: an old, owl-faced rare-book collector with tiny round glasses, a long white beard, and hair to match; a perpetually furious librarian who hushed and scolded children— even those on their best behavior; and, of course, there were the eccentric and unpredictable dealers (who were rather nice once you knew them) in shops so old you could still smell the books on your clothes days later. To a young reader, these memorable people became indelible parts of the stories that they lovingly passed along.

My father first came to New York in July 1968. Though still a teenager, he had sold drawings to the *New Yorker* that would eventually appear on the magazine's cover. After that, he would visit frequently, staying with his mother's friends on Madison Avenue, directly across from the Morgan Library. He spent his days discovering classic Midtown and Uptown stores like Ursus, Argosy, and Swann, and still today fondly recalls the legendary Gotham Book Mart in the Diamond District—the same place he held his first New York exhibition in 1977.

Decades later, I moved to New York and was instinctively drawn to exploring the city's literary secrets. The skyline was certainly different from the versions my father had depicted, but much of what makes New York a special place for curious bibliophiles is still here. I found a library inside a subway station (The Terence Cardinal Cooke-Cathedral Library); at least eighteen miles of books in a space so charming you will find it hard to leave (Strand); a bookshop open after nightfall with a shady corridor packed with secondhand undiscovered art and photobooks (Mercer Street Books & Records); and the dark-wood booth in which Madeline—my all-time favorite character—was created (Pete's Tavern).

Even after years living in New York—the epicenter of belletristic brilliance and cultural abundance—my quest for uncovering everything book-related only grows more rewarding. The results of this endless search are captured here, in *A Booklover's Guide to New York*.

THE FINANCIAL DISTRICT, TRIBECA, CHINATOWN & THE LOWER EAST SIDE

At the very southern tip of Manhattan, you will find some of the island's most fabled and historically important neighborhoods. The South Street Seaport was once home to the most significant wholesale East Coast fish market in the United States. The Fulton Fish Market has moved to the Bronx, but its original building is still in place. It is now home to 10 Corso Como—a far cry from the old fishmonger stands—where you can buy art and fashion books among curated designer goods. Some of Downtown Manhattan's oldest architecture still adorns the Seaport's quiet cobblestone streets.

To the southwest of the neighborhood, you will quickly run into the FiDi (the Financial District) and all its mysterious office towers and condominiums, which one can only imagine hide seedy lost characters, from Bret Easton Ellis's infamous Patrick Bateman to the nameless and debauched hero of Jay McInerney's *Bright Lights, Big City*. Just north, City Hall, the Woolworth Building, and the Thurgood Marshall and Tweed Courthouses mark the territory once known as Five Points—a region filled with both notoriety and historical significance, all documented in Herbert Asbury's *The Gangs of New York*. A few blocks west is TriBeCa (the Triangle Below Canal Street) with its soaring lofts, high-end stores, and wandering parents and prams.

Head east from TriBeCa and you will stumble into a personal favourite: Chinatown, which is still such an authentic, raw, smelly, grimy, fun, and bustling hub of activity that nobody should ever pass by. Adjacent to Chinatown's crowded and noisy streets, a blurry frontier separates the dim sum parlors from the LES (Lower East Side), with its gritty streets filled with trendy bars, small indie boutiques, and new galleries. The Jewish, Irish, and Italian pioneers who settled these neighborhoods would hardly recognize much of this area today. Beyond its gentrification, though, you will uncover the LES's rich history through its fascinating tenement buildings, many of which are thankfully still standing—and some of them even sell books.

The Mysterious Bookshop
58 Warren Street

My first stop on this literary journey had to be the one and only mystery bookshop in New York. Relocated from Midtown in 2005, to far downtown, the Mysterious Bookshop specializes in mystery, crime, and espionage titles, and is something of a secret itself. Once discovered, this shop is an extraordinary place to find in a city where independent bookstores seem to be "mysteriously" vanishing.

Situated on Warren Street in TriBeCa—within walking distance of the offices where Edgar Allan Poe imagined gruesome tales during his day job at the *Evening Mirror*—the Mysterious Book-shop is a haven for any crime, suspense, and thriller reader in search of a signed copy of the latest best seller, an old noir classic, or even a vintage secondhand paperback with a sexy pinup on its cover (some of which are available for close to pennies!). This welcoming and homey destination is also somewhat of a safe house for any celebrity or anonymous mystery author, savvy crime collector, or even just a regular fan of the genre. As well as stocking everything from the new school of macabre Scandinavian thrillers to rare and collectible editions of Victorian penny dreadfuls, the store is famous for hosting book signings for authors, from the up-and-coming to the very well-known. It also has its very own Bibliomystery series—a collection of crime novellas set in and around the literary world, written exclusively for the store and published in limited quantities monthly.

Whether you are a crime fiction virgin (like myself), an avid collector looking to join one of the store's book clubs, or an old-school religious reader of Agatha Christie and John le Carré, the Mysterious Bookshop has something to pique your (criminal) curiosity.

Otto Penzler

Owner of the Mysterious Bookshop,
founder of *The Mysterious Press*,
editor of mystery fiction, and
number-one figure at the
forefront of the mystery fiction
industry in the United States

How did you first come about opening the Mysterious Bookshop?

I started a publishing company, The Mysterious Press, in 1975. Our first books came out in 1976. It was a one-person company (me), so I was acquiring books, negotiating the contracts, editing, hiring an artist to do the jackets, writing flap copy, sending out review copies, taking orders, doing the banking, packing up the books and shipping them. It was fine until I had success, and then it was impossible to keep up.

I tried to find an apartment in Manhattan with an extra room that I could use as an office, so I could get secretarial help. I had no money, and I was living in the Bronx. I looked around and couldn't afford the rents, so I ended up buying a building on 56th Street, right behind Carnegie Hall. Then I had all this space, and thought, "Wouldn't it be fun to open a bookshop?" I knew nothing about having a bookshop. The bookshop opened on Friday, April 13, 1979. I was there for twenty-six years—I had a partner—then we sold the building and moved to TriBeCa.

It was a whim. I've always loved books. I've been a reader and a collector. Then I had this space and just thought how great it would be to have a shop, without knowing anything about owning a shop. But I knew nothing about publishing when I started either, so . . . That's how it started.

Was it a big and popular market back in the 1970s?

No, it was very niche. It took until the mid-1980s for it to become much bigger. One of the things that changed it is that women started writing more hard-boiled fiction—Sue Grafton, Sara Paretsky, and others became hugely popular. It attracted more women to the store, not just to read but also to collect first editions of those books. Collecting is a huge part of our store and our business, and when collectors started including women, it became a very substantial part of the business.

Were mystery and crime rampant at the time in New York?

Real-life crime? Yes. Last year there were fewer than three hundred murders in New York City. In the 1970s, it was averaging twenty-five hundred a year. There were streets you would not walk on after it turned dark. Central Park—you would never go near it after it was dark. Ninth and Tenth Avenues—you would never go there either.

Is the mystery fiction world very separate from the literary scene?

I've labored for close to forty years to break down that barrier between the two. When I publish books I have an imprint at Grove Atlantic, The Mysterious Press is now part of it, and I publish literary crime fiction—people like Robert Olen Butler, who's a Pulitzer Prize–winner, and Joyce Carol Oates, who I think is probably the best living writer who hasn't won a Nobel Prize. So I love literary crime fiction and I think mysteries should have the same standards as other fiction in terms of style, originality, character development, and so on. A lot of literary crime fiction and mystery is junk, but often it's not.

What qualifies as mystery fiction?

For me, any work of fiction in which the crime or the threat of a crime is integral to the plot, is a mystery.

What makes for a good mystery?

What makes a good mystery is the same as what makes good literature: poetic writing style, a fascinating character who comes alive on the page, writing that uses language or dialogue that you've never heard used the same way before, something original, interesting background, something colorful in the background . . . all the criteria that you would use for literature, you would use for crime fiction. Except in addition to that, you need to have a serious plot. Often literature is superbly written but not much happens and there is sometimes no real plot. Good mystery fiction is harder to write than general fiction.

What is your favorite unsolved mystery?

The black dahlia murder case in Los Angeles. A girl's body was found in a parking lot cut in half and eviscerated, and it was never solved. It became the subject of my first *New York Times*–best-selling book called *The Black Dahlia*. The mystery was simply never solved, and the author, James Ellroy, also lost his mother to an unsolved crime.

How close have you come to being like a mystery-fiction character?

Oh, I don't do anything to be like a mystery-fiction character—but I have been an actual character. Authors have put me in their books. They use me frequently, and some change my name. Nelson DeMille used me as Oscar Parker, for example. Elmore Leonard used me as Otto Penzler, in two of his books, I believe.

Have you noticed a change in trends in the mystery fiction genre over the years?

There have been several trends in the past forty years that I have been in the business. First, nowadays, there is greater respect for mysteries. Back in the day, people would walk in and say, "I don't read mystery, I'm getting this for my uncle." So I would say, "Oh you've never read Dostoevsky?" and then they'd say, "Of course I've read him," and I'd answer, "Well, *Crime and Punishment* is a crime novel." They'd try and say they didn't think of it like that, but I would say to them, "Well you should."

As time has gone by, there is less snobbery about it, for two reasons. Mystery writers (the better ones) have become much more literary and pay much more attention to style. People like Dennis Lehane, Michael Connelly, Daniel Woodrell, and George Pelecanos, to name a few, are true literary writers.

On the other side, literary writers like Joyce Carol Oates or Robert Olen Butler have started to incorporate crime and mystery into their fiction, and there is a lot of that on both sides. That was a major trend. The blending of those two trends is the most important thing that has happened in the past forty years.

The influx of writing by women started in the early 1980s, and that is still going strong. It did not exist before. Now, obviously, it's a given, and people do not think about gender anymore in the industry.

Would you say there is a big community of mystery writers, sellers, and dealers in New York?
Yes, quite. This is the place, I would say. Tonight, for example, we are having a signing with an author who has written his second book, but he will be interviewed by Megan Abbott, who is a very successful mystery writer, and other mystery writers will come to the event to be supportive. There is also the Mystery Writers of America—their New York Chapter is here. They do monthly dinner cocktail parties for mystery writers, publishers, and editors who all attend the event. There is quite a bit of that going on. This is ground zero.

Cookbooks
488 Greenwich Street

A dear friend who lives in TriBeCa once showed me a photo of a beautifully tarnished wooden door with an old-fashioned metal plaque inscribed with the simple word: Cookbooks. It was the front door to a secret and magical little shop I had never heard of.

Said friend described the place as a cute little ground-floor room with cookbooks, oddities, and small objects displayed on an organized mess of divine shelves. I immediately looked it up, and it seemed to be in a suitably isolated location and open to the public on a somewhat irregular basis. I quickly realized this might have something to do with the fact that the charming owner, Joanne Hendricks, lives above the shop in the gorgeous nineteenth-century townhouse that hosts it. I thought it would be best to call up Hendricks to ask when I could pay a visit.

"Well, you see, we aren't always open every day. But when I'm in town, we are sometimes here at all hours, so just call ahead and come in." Hendricks mentioned she was going to Vermont soon; so the next day I trotted down to TriBeCa and was not disappointed. Cookbooks was as mesmerizing as I expected, if not more so. I was completely transported into Hendricks's personal, exuberant, and enchanting world—a culinary and visually impressive library of sorts that I quickly became infatuated with.

Joanne Hendricks

Owner of Cookbooks, and
lives above the shop in a
nineteenth-century house
in TriBeCa

How did you first open this shop? What was the inspiration behind it?

In 1995, there was a downstairs front room in our house that screamed, "Make me a shop again!" I live in an early nineteenth-century house with lots of New York history. But I lived in a neighborhood with few neighbors, cobbled streets, trucks and private carters, warehouses, no food stores—it was a waterfront and quiet. A wonderful place to open a cookbook shop, a used and antiquarian cookbook shop.

How did you come about specializing in food books? Was it always a passion?

At the time I opened my shop I was a young mother, sewing, cooking, knitting, and reading books about food and households. I was reading books on those subjects and looking at the bibliographies in them—tangents in different directions. I admired Eleanor Lowenstein, Tessa McKirdy, and bookshop owners.

Are you a chef or simply a collector of beautiful books?

A bit of both. I cook all the time. I have a limited palate, but I love books and collecting them. I'm thrilled to find something rare and special and beautiful.

The bookshop feels so homey and personal. I know you live above the shop, but do you consider it part of your home?

This is my home. The rolls of wallpaper were stored in an attic in my husband's family's home. It was there for many years and I thought it might look nice. Also I do bring my husband and daughters and their families and pets to my shop.

What is the rarest or most extraordinary book you have ever acquired?

I had a beautiful, early Japanese scroll in two colors with meat-cutting diagrams. I also had a very nice collection of Shaker ephemera, which I sold to a dealer who also bought an early manuscript book of recipes, which was dated 1703. I have so many special books, newer and older, and had so many that were sold that it's difficult to name just one. It saddens me to part with some books.

Do a lot of chefs come and buy books in your shop? Who is your favorite New York chef?

I do have a number of chefs coming to my shop. I know this because they tell me they are chefs. Jody Williams has a restaurant called Buvette in Greenwich Village. She popularized artichokes Judaica. I like her menu. But I love, love, love good old-fashioned short-order cooks at a diner, and I get plenty of those in the store, too.

Has the new wave of "foodie" culture and celebrity chefs affected your area of work, or impacted the domain of more classic cookery books?

That I couldn't answer. I hope the foodies have libraries they use as references before they invent a new dish.

What's the most literary anecdote you have about food or cooking?

If I may name an entire novel, it would be *Mrs. Dalloway* by Virginia Woolf. And before Bourdain capitalized on George Orwell's *Down and Out in Paris and London* and forever claimed it as his own (R.I.P.), that book was another favorite of mine. *My Ántonia* by Willa Cather has many food references in it. Cather was a good American author.

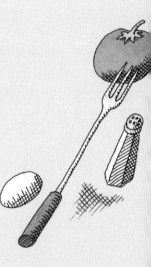

Aside from your shop, what's another great place to get books in the city?

The Strand is a great place to find books—but the store is getting too neat looking. Bonnie Slotnick sells a lot of great cookbooks, too.

Given your specialty and expertise, what's the best place to get food for you in New York?

I go to Di Palo's on Grand Street for ravioli and cheeses and olive oil. Pino's on Sullivan Street is my butcher. Piemonte on Grand Street is where I buy dried macaroni and spaghetti. I often get good fruit in Chinatown, in the winter only, and oranges for juicing. Bread at Breads Bakery on 16th Street. I also do a lot of shopping at farms in Vermont when I'm up there—and I have planted a vegetable garden.

If there was one book you haven't gotten yet and you would love to get, what would it be?

Maybe a little late sixteenth- or early seventeenth-century book of simples. Indeed, I would love anything written by a Queen or a Lady—*The Queen's Closet Opened.*

Poets House
10 River Terrace

If you head nearly all the way south, by the water, on the west side of the island, there is a strange little part of Manhattan which, although only developed in the 1980s, I very much enjoy. I am usually more of an appreciator of old neighborhoods, but I make exceptions when it is for the greater good. That greater good could involve comfort, culture, interesting activities . . . Down by Battery Park there is a little bit of all of that: a multiplex cinema to revel in (with seats that recline fully horizontal, and lots of escalators to get around on), a lovely and open park that children appreciate greatly, sporty types of activities I absolutely do not engage in, nice paths by the water to walk along, and, most relevant here, the Poets House.

After recently celebrating its thirtieth anniversary, the Poets House still prides itself on bringing world-renowned poets to new audiences. Founded in 1985 by Stanley Kunitz (U.S. Poet Laureate) and Elizabeth Kray (an arts administrator), the Poets House serves millions of poetry fans by documenting modern poetry and exposing the world to its beauty.

After twenty years in SoHo, Poets House is now at the base of the Riverhouse condominium tower in a giant location that houses children's activities, special exhibits and events, workshops, and a library of seventy thousand poetry volumes. It is free, open to the public, and a great place whether you are well versed in poetry or a novice in search of a poetic urban retreat for a calm moment.

Eddie Huang

Author, chef, and TV personality

Eddie Huang

You started off as a chef, then became a TV host and personality, then an author. What made you go through all these transitions?

Well, I always wanted to write stories and direct films. That was the dream. My brother, Emery, and I felt like aliens as kids and really connected with characters in comics, books, and movies. My parents fought pretty violently at home. When it went down, I'd hide Emery under the bed or build a fort out of a sofa, and we'd pretend to be X-Men. That's why I started telling stories: I was trying to manifest an invincibility to everything falling apart around me. Eventually I fell apart myself in adulthood, but fuck it, I'll write about my next move too.

I love food, and it was the way I was allowed to tell stories in this country. People didn't want stories from Chinamen, they laughed at me when I turned in screenplays with Chinese or Caribbean characters—I grew up working in my dad's restaurant with Caribbean dudes—and was told no one would ever make movies with "these people." But I saw that they wanted food from "these people," so I opened Baohaus and told stories through food. Eventually I made my way back to what I wanted to do in the first place: writing.

What is the most gratifying part of writing your own books?

I am working on my first novel now. Fiction has been really liberating. I never had a problem telling my own story, but it's hard when other people are involved. Sometimes you accept what's happened before your family or friends have, and it's tough to write if the emotions aren't fully baked for everyone. That is a funny thing about writing, and I just accept it.

I think the most gratifying part of writing is the emotional release. You can physically feel your spirit giving this energy back to the universe. Sometimes it feels like I'm going around and around on this ride that only stops when I come to terms with my condition and existence. When I can do that in my writing, the world stops and it feels like I'm fulfilling some greater purpose. Then some other shit happens and you're back on the ride learning a new lesson. I know I sound like a kook that sells crystals and throws full moon parties, but it's probably because I be that.

What is your writing process like? Where do you like to write when you are in New York?

Havoc had this line once, "I'm a gemini bitch / that mean I flip with the weather." My writing process flips with the project. Every project has a different flow and energy, but I really commit to it. There's usually a friend or hobby or curiosity that I can connect to every project, and really drove it. I wrote the proposal for *Fresh Off the Boat* over one weekend in an apartment on Norfolk Street over the original Baohaus. When I sold the book, I took the bread and moved Baohaus to 14th Street, then got an apartment with my brother, Evan, in Stuytown. I would check in at the restaurant early, but Evan handled the business so I could write. I owe him a lot.

That sense of duty and responsibility to my brother and ancestors drove that process. I wrote the first draft in three months and sat at the same desk every day for eight to twelve hours. The energy with *Fresh Off the Boat* was pure immigrant survival. I remember sending progress every day to Evan and my best friend, Rafael—in case anything happened to me they had it and could finish it. There was a desperation to get my family's and people's story out. That book wrote itself; it was my grandparents, my parents, my brothers, and friends who carried me. All I had to do was sit in the chair and it poured out. Lots of people sacrificed for that record. Ha! I would always call it a record, too, because as I got older I got more from music than books.

The only writer I fucked with besides the OGs was Junot Díaz at that time. After I sent in my first draft, Chris Jackson told me to read *The Brief Wondrous Life of Oscar Wao*. It bugged me out that he existed, and I stopped reading after fifty pages because son was in my head. First thing I did after finishing *Fresh Off the Boat* was read *Oscar Wao*. It's my favorite book. I still read a lot of Shakespeare for fun, but Junot is Yoda to me.

You've been characterized as a provocative and combative writer at times. Why?

Probably because I am. It's fight night when I write. It doesn't interest me to write about commonly accepted topics or ideas. I get my juju from saying things that I feel will have a positive impact on the world, and that usually requires challenging people. Socrates always said he was the "Gadfly of Athens," and I took that to heart. I read *A Midsummer Night's Dream* constantly because it reminds writers and audiences of their duty to the universe. This isn't escape, this isn't entertainment—it's the work. I hate when writers and artists or "creatives" fetishize their work and want people to feel them just because they're "creating." I look at a lot of this shit and I'm like, "what are you teaching me? How are you challenging me?" A lot of "creative" work is trash right now, because it's about garnering likes. That's totally in opposition to what art is supposed to do. Art should challenge and inspire you to grow and change and fulfill your commitment to the universe and everything in it.

Do the books you read reflect your professional passions and projects? What book do you bring when you travel the world reporting?

I think about books like ghosts. I start a lot of books and don't finish them because they're ghosts I don't want to talk to. Recently, I've read a lot of Ha Jin. I'm feeling everything that ghost is talking about and it really put a spell on me earlier this year. I'm trying to find something new at the moment, but really I've just listened to a lot of Max B tapes. That's who I'm writing to now. Music affects my writing just as much as books. I will put one song on repeat for hours so I can stay in a rhythm.

What was your favorite book as a kid? Did you and your friends read a lot?
I really liked the autobiography of Hank Aaron, *I Had A Hammer,* and *Thank you, Jackie Robinson*; I copped almost all the Matt Christopher sports books, and *Goosebumps.* I read a lot about race, especially from the black perspective, because black people resisted globally. They refused to accept what people were doing to them. Same for Jewish people. I went to a Yeshiva school and was really inspired by their resistance and perseverance. Same for early Irish immigrants. I wish white immigrants remembered what they went through and had more empathy for immigrants today. In the Asian-American community, I saw a lot of yielding and submitting, which I couldn't relate to, so I turned to older texts like *Romance of the Three Kingdoms* and Fifth Wave Chinese Cinema about the cultural revolution and its aftermath. I love reading about Ethiopia, Jamaica, Haiti, Cuba, Anne Frank, *Star Wars,* Zhang Yimou films . . .

I read a ton of comics. I liked the Punisher and Batman because they really didn't want to accept evil in the world. I hated all the inequality and pain I was seeing, so I lived vicariously through Punisher and Batman. *The Dark Knight* was a favorite, and the Punisher issue where he shoots up a wedding. Spawn was dope, too. I liked the dudes that got fucked by the world and refused to die.

You're a food expert. Where do you get your cookbooks in New York City? Where do you get books in Chinatown?
At this point, people send me cookbooks, but the ones I actually use are all from the Taipei 101 bookstore. When I go to Taipei, I cop a lot of books. I grew up learning from my mom. Every once in a while, we peeped P. E. Mei. She was the first to write in Chinese-English, so much respect to her and her daughter, who got fire books too. I wouldn't recommend buying cookbooks from any of these new-jack Chinese chefs, they're kinda booty. The techniques and ratios are five thousand years old. That's the core of every cuisine: master the technique and ratios. The ingredients all have a relationship to each other and the ratios or proportions are like their I-Ching. French wine is the greatest, because it's been documented and demarcated for thousands of years by monks. Nothing surprises these cats. A lot of these people don't study them and pay respect. They're just making Chinese food or wine off the top of the dome, and it's a mess. Hubris drives me crazy. I've always been a student of the game . . . every game.

How would you define your style and cultural identity? If you could pick one, what book would you use as a sort of bible to best reflect that?
Fresh Off the Boat is kind of my bible for the first third of my life, but the books I really

connect with are: *Batman: The Dark Knight Returns*, *Julius Caesar*, *The Brief Wondrous Life of Oscar Wao*, and *Waiting* by Ha Jin.

I've heard people say you're better at being a TV personality and author than a cook. What is your reaction to that?
Ha! Yeah, people front on my cooking until they get invited to dinner, but they shut the fuck up real quick when the rice flour spareribs come out. There are one or two people writing about food that actually need to be heard. The rest are just dumbasses with iPhones and bylines.

That's why I don't invite food press to my dinners unless the brands make me. You can't invite Pete Wells or Ligaya Mishan, anyway, and they're the only ones I respect. R.I.P. Jonathan Gold. I don't think Besha Rodell writes anymore, and she was great. I talk to Yu Bo and Andy Ricker about food when something excites me. Nick Jammet at Sweetgreen is super interesting to talk to about the business of it all. Internet food journalism might be the greatest crime committed against words. The landscape is littered with failed music and fashion writers descending on a culture they've never worked in or submitted themselves to. You have to give yourself to something before you have anything to say. A lot of people want to talk, but aren't giving us shit.

How has the foodie scene changed over the years?
Food culture is washed. I just go to the same old restaurants. Waiting for the Jedi to return.

What's the most precious book that you've ever been in possession of?
I have a Manny Pacquiao–signed copy of Jane Jacobs's *Death and Life of Great American Cities*. I also have a Tom Brady–signed copy of *Slouching Towards Bethlehem*.

What extravagant or hideous color would you repaint your library shelves in?
Ha! I love money green or pistachio.

Seward Park Library
192 East Broadway

There is something very official about the way this grand building stands on the edge of Seward Park—the friendly, local, and rare piece of Chinatown greenery after which the library was named. The park housed the first permanent, municipally built playground in the country, and was named after William H. Seward, former U.S. Secretary of State and Governor of New York—a strong unionist who fought against the spread of slavery and survived an assassination attempt during the same plot that killed Abraham Lincoln.

In the summer, the library is a (rather strongly) air-conditioned sanctum set away from the scorching heat, the invisible (but oh-so-present) rats, and the overbearing Chinatown crowds. The building itself, which dates all the way back to 1886, is quite glorious and imposing; and the library is spread over four floors, most of them open to the public. All the way in the far southern Lower East Side, the library served an immigrant Jewish population in its very early days.

As you walk in, the first floor feels like a sort of junior high school hall of bustling activities: huge groups of kids can be found sitting at circular tables, most of them with big backpacks thrown over their shoulders, comparing video games, comics, or whatever new gadgets they have with them. It is sweet and cheerful, but a little too noisy for my liking, and a difficult place to study or be productive in that "library" sort of way. Climb up to either the second floor (for kids) or third (for adults), and you will find your peace.

Everything about this library branch is accommodating: spacious tables with ample plugs for your laptops, all categories of books arranged neatly, and (as I found out when I stumbled into an adult knitting club) classes and other events scheduled throughout the week. Opened at its current location back in 1909, this branch has truly kept its standards. It is not only a pleasure to use this library for books and study; it can actually come in very handy when you are in search of some serenity or find yourself a wandering soul in Manhattan's busy Lower East Side. (As a side note, I also hope all those ground-floor kids stay right where they are. They do not just add to this library's charm; they make it a lively, warm, and inviting hub of activity where neighborhood locals can gather.)

Richardson
325 Broome Street

Walk back west to the more gentrified side of the neighborhood (funnily enough, closer to the Bowery) and you will find a little shop called Richardson. You could easily miss it, as it is slightly above street level—walk up half a dozen stoop stairs, though, and you will see its neon "R" and smell the Japanese incense burning within.

The shop is owned by Andrew Richardson, a former (rather successful) fashion stylist who created the eponymous magazine *Richardson*, which has some elements of pornography or eroticism (depending on who's looking and obviously what you're looking at) within it, but is also a highly respected cultural publication. He recently developed a streetwear brand of the same name, which everybody—from my traditional, not-very-trendy husband to my über-hipster fashion-obsessed little brother—absolutely loves. When the shop opened, it was only natural for Richardson also to sell books. The selection is varied, but most of it is either deeply intellectual, aesthetically pleasing, or highly sophisticated.

It was best to hear all about it from the man himself; Richardson the person, not the magazine or the shop.

Andrew Richardson

Former fashion stylist and consultant,
publisher of the magazine *Richardson,*
owner of the successful streetwear brand
Richardson and two Richardson
stores, in Los Angeles and New York

Your magazine Richardson *features a lot of sex but also other cultural topics, and now you have a successful streetwear brand of the same name. How does your personal library, as well as the book selection in your New York shop, reflect that?*
The book selection in my shop is specific to the interests that relate to the magazine. My personal library is broader. Now that the magazine is collaborating with Magnum, we can expand the perimeters of the magazine and expand the book selection in the shop, so that it is less erotic.

Are there any erotic bookshops in New York? Would you say your book section is what comes closest? What other books do well in the shop?
To my knowledge, there are no existing erotic bookshops in New York. At the New York Art Book Fair there is usually a man with a lot of erotic material, which is very good, but I cannot think of his name.

Books that do well in my shop are punk books, like Toby Mott's *Showboat,* and a few other counterculture and antiestablishment ones do well, too—which is where erotic books come from.

What would be the go-to erotic book to get a beginner, or a person who has never had any erotic books, as a gift?
John Willie's *The Adventures of Sweet Gwendoline* would be the best book to start with, because it is erotic but it is beautifully rendered and done in very good taste. Willie provided a bridge between more extreme erotic European illustrations from the 1890s to the 1930s (which used to be privately traded in smoking rooms among aristocratic circles in Germany, France, and Italy), made it more palatable, and dialed it down from some of the weird psychology. He created something exciting and accessible. He was the bridge between the underground erotic world and the more mainstream artists in the late 1940s. Then came people like Bettie Page and Irving Klaw.

What type of books do you read for work? What do you read for pleasure? And how do they differ?
I end up reading a lot of books like Iceberg Slim's *Pimp: The Story of My Life* or Thorstein Veblen's *The Theory of the Leisure Class.* The next book I am reading is *Testo Junkie* by Paul B. Preciado—it is about sex, drugs, and biopolitics in the pharmaco-pornographic era. Everything I read is usually to develop my own personal culture, which ends up getting translated in the magazine.

Keith Haring used to live in the building where the Richardson shop is now. How did you find out about that? Do you have any stories or anecdotes about it?

He lived on the third floor of the building where the shop is, and his painting studio was in the basement. If you go to the lampshade store under my shop, there is a wall on which they only used a thin coat of paint over the walls, and you can see Keith Haring and Jean-Michel Basquiat tags on the wall under the paint.

The guy I rented the shop and floor above from only rented to artists, so the Richardson shop actually used to be Maya Lin's studio. There were also doors and beams in the building that had Haring's radiant babies on them, and the owner sold them for a lot of money.

You partake in the New York Art Book Fair. What do you think about it? What is it doing for young creatives and the younger "arty" book scene in New York? How has that scene changed since you first moved here?

I like it. Established sellers that show there have great books that you wouldn't normally see in the same space all together. There are also rooms with zines and smaller publications, where you get to see what kids are doing—there are often odd weird gems in there. You get to see great current new-release books and people from all over the world. There is a wide selection of books all in one place—old and new ones, and good ones, too—and it is inspiring to find new ideas for the magazine there. The "scene" used to be more antisocial, aggressive, and exciting. It is now more politically correct and socially conscious. New York is "woke," which is a necessary thing, but people do provocative and antagonizing things less and less.

If you wrote an erotic novel, where in New York would you set it? And what street would the main character live on?

I would not set it in New York, but if I had to I would set it on Forsyth between Broome and Delancey streets. The main character would live there, at my place.

Where is the best place to acquire (buy, borrow, or find) a book on the Lower East Side?

Dashwood Books and Mast Books.

What's the most precious (in rarity, or monetary or sentimental value) book that you've ever been in possession of?

I have an incredible copy of Christer Strömholm's *Poste Restante*, which is signed and worth a lot. I also have a pristine copy of Daido Moriyama's *Farewell Photography*, which is my favorite book of all time.

What is the sexiest way to enjoy a good book?

In a candlelit bath.

What extravagant or fun color would you repaint your shop in?

Safety green.

Tenement Museum
103 Orchard Street

For a short while, I was a (far) Downtown resident, and there was always a lot of controversy among my peers and others as to whether I actually lived in Chinatown or on the Lower East Side. Many years later, I would still be incapable of defining where the border between those two areas actually is.

What I do know is that around the corner from where I lived was the Tenement Museum, a place that was already very popular when I first moved there and whose popularity has only grown since. Crowds would amass at every which hour and for every tour. They would peruse the neighborhood in large groups, listening to a guide, and sometimes asking questions about this or that building, the alleyway down there, and what used to be here and who lived up in there. Even my ninety-something-year-old grandparents wanted to come all the way down from Central Park just to go to the museum. (In all fairness, though, they are immigrants of Ashkenazi heritage, they love history, and my grandmother has often been known to enjoy walking around in big tourist groups, so I guess it was justified.)

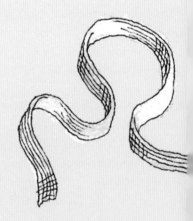

Personally, I never really cared for the idea of a tour guide explaining my own neighborhood to me—but I do truly respect the museum's original idea, the institution it has become, and the values for which it stands. And what I did find myself visiting quite regularly during my tenure in the neighborhood was the Tenement Museum's gift shop. It has a surprisingly large collection of books, specializing mainly in the neighborhood's history and culture as well as New York as a city, its rich heritage, and its very important and diverse immigrant population. The shop also has a great selection of children's books. Many of these make perfect gifts, whether for the seasoned New Yorker, history-hungry new arrival, or curious visitor.

Perrotin Bookstore
130 Orchard Street

Emmanuel Perrotin opened his first gallery in Paris in 1990, and shortly afterward began representing Takashi Murakami and Maurizio Cattelan, a decade before they were world-renowned artists. Since those early days, Perrotin has successfully opened eighteen different spaces and currently makes use of 75,000 square feet of gallery space world-wide, filled with precious, innovative, and fun contemporary art. He continues to work with young artists who go on to become household names such as KAWS and JR. I'll always remember a deal I made with Perrotin when I was seven years old; I traded a small drawing of a rather sad-looking bicycle my dad had left with me for a secondhand—first generation, I might add—Nintendo Game Boy. (Video games were expressly forbidden and I was absolutely delighted.)

His latest American endeavor is in the gigantic old S. Beckenstein upholstery and fabric building, which Perrotin reimagined into one of his spectacular galleries in 2017. As with most good galleries, a bookshop completes this Downtown staple, and this one should by no means be overlooked.

The shop is not only packed with interesting books (of personal favorites like Sophie Calle, Farhad Moshiri, and Xavier Veilhan), it also sells affordable (and sometimes a little less affordable) artist editions, as well as unusual and rather amusing goodies one would be delighted to receive as gifts. Then there are Perrotin Editions: catalogues of exhibitions the gallery hosted for its artists, including Daniel Arsham, Erró, Hans Hartung, Jean-Michel Othoniel and, of course, Takashi Murakami. If you are looking for an arty treat or a bit of contemporary Japanese, French, or international food for thought, the Orchard Street Perrotin Bookstore should definitely be a stop on your LES circuit.

Bluestockings
172 Allen Street

In the 1750s, two Elizabeths (Montagu and Vesey) founded an informal social and educational movement called the Blue Stockings Society. As a literary discussion group made for women and founded by women, the Blue Stockings Society was completely revolutionary—at the time, women were typically expected to engage in more traditional, non-intellectual activities.

It was only natural for this very engaged, collectively owned, and volunteer-powered bookstore to be named after the English eighteenth-century movement. Conveniently located since 1999 in a huge and very open space on one of the most busy streets of the Lower East Side, the shop is home to thousands of books, mostly themed around "radical" topics such as feminism, gender studies, global capitalism, climate, environment, race, prisons, and a long list of other issues for which the owners have a passion.

The shop also has a café with all sorts of organic, fair-trade, and vegan treats. And with such a welcoming space, it makes sense that the store would host lots of interesting events, from readings to book signings and lectures, all of which are open to the public.

10 Corso Como
1 Fulton Street

All the way down in Manhattan's South Street Seaport, the über-fashionable 10 Corso Como megastore set up shop in 2018. Located in what was once the Fulton Fish Market building, the 28,000-square-foot space certainly lives up to the historic neighborhood's expectations. All laid out on the ex-market's ground floor, the shop fully awakens all shoppers' visual, intellectual, and even epicurean senses. With 10 Corso Como's signature look (imagined by the artist Kris Ruhs, who also created the artwork for all the other international 10 Corso Como shops), the setting transports you into a new world, both unexpected and somewhat magical—and certainly unique among the Seaport district's existing offerings. Along with a restaurant, a gallery, and a gigantic array of high-end items such as clothes, accessories, and design pieces, the opulent book department of 10 Corso Como houses a wide variety of art, design, and fashion literature—perfectly chosen to satisfy any chic and cultivated customer. The bookstore area is to the left (just before the café restaurant) after the main entrance, and is a lovely setting for some low-key, pleasant, literary browsing. Grab a book and settle with some spaghetti in the restaurant, and you can reflect on the exquisite details of the 10 Corso Como universe.

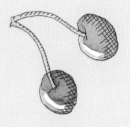

SOHO, NOHO & NOLITA

Circa 1890, the legendary bookseller George D. Smith opened a bookstore on Fourth Avenue, which marked the beginning of what would soon become a world-famous territory of six blocks that went by the name of Book Row. From that period in time up until about the 1960s, almost every shopfront on Fourth Avenue between Union Square and Astor Place—where the famed Astor Library once held court—was a secondhand bookshop.

Tragically, Book Row no longer exists, but there are a few remnants of it scattered around the city: the Strand, which used to be on Book Row, is now around the corner on Broadway; Argosy, which moved up to East 59th Street; and the many tales of how Book Row is so sorely missed and how fondly cherished and adored it used to be.

South of the Book Row region is NoHo (North of Houston), where one can leisurely stroll wide and airy pavements, while visiting cool shops such as the ever-so-popular Dashwood Books. If you miss the crowds, though, head a little south to SoHo (South of Houston), where artists and authors still live and create in oversized, beautiful, and quintessentially New York cast-iron lofts.

McNally Jackson

52 Prince Street
76 North 4th Street, Brooklyn

McNally Jackson is a bookstore's bookstore, a shop with its own literary family history. Owned by Sarah McNally, the daughter of the founders of the successful major Canadian bookstore chain McNally Robinson, the shop manages to bring together serious literary chops with trendy Downtown cool.

Very centrally located on the ever-so-slightly more quiet side of Prince Street (east of Broadway), it also has a café, which serves breakfast-type food as well as hot and cold beverages during the day and whose seats are re-arranged to accommodate readings and signings by night. Aside from its two airy floors of very well-presented and aesthetically pleasant shelves of books—with fiction unusually organized by the nationality of author—there is also a whole area downstairs with kids' books, history titles, and a newly installed bargain section. In addition, a vast selection of all sorts of international magazines can be discreetly flicked through, if you need to check something out before you commit to buying it. The really cool notebooks and pens (among many other unusual accessories) from all over the world (mostly awesome Japanese versions of old-school French journals and notebooks—you'll understand when you see them) makes it difficult to leave the shop without buying something. I went in for a quick browse and to check some facts for my research, and left with a miniature leather envelope I have no idea how I will use.

Everything for sale here is either super-cute or mega-cool, and if the store weren't so distinctively New York in its own special kind of SoHo way, you could easily picture yourself at a mall in Tokyo's Ginza. The fact that it is open until 10 p.m. most days makes it that much more difficult to leave! The McNally Jackson empire extends to a few other equally charming locations—stationery and design stores on Mulberry and West 8th streets, and a brilliant new bookshop in Williamsburg.

Mulberry Street Library
10 Jersey Street

This is where it all started. A few years ago I had been working on a novel based on my family's history—all the good and the bad through the troubled lens of a teenage girl's mind. Everything was there, and all I needed was to go over it, and, I guess, finish it. Not to go on about my personal life, but I had definitely learned and appreciated (via a small but quite cool university) that libraries are the best places to get stuff done. So that is where I decided I needed to go. I searched for the library closest to where I was staying at the time, and there it was: the Mulberry Street branch of the New York Public Library.

Though it's officially named the Mulberry Street Library, I call it the Jersey Street one. Possibly because I like to make sure absolutely nobody knows about this place, but maybe also because I have such a fond attachment to it; I wanted to give it its own personal little nickname. Few people know this, but whenever I need to finish something, I go and hide in the second basement of this magical building, which used to be a chocolate factory.

That is what I love so much about this library: all the way down in the basement levels of an old chocolate factory, you truly feel like you can concentrate in all anonymity. Discreet and on a side street (in fact it almost seems to only be half a street) which easily goes unnoticed, the building is modern looking and, for a European, completely lacks charm—if you decide to ignore one of their most regular customers. He's an older-looking man who always has a big paparazzi-esque camera and looks like he is (still) in a punk-rock band. And that is precisely why I hold this dear library so close to my heart: for its diversity, its utility, and its humor that sneaks up on you when you least expect it.

This library gave me absolutely everything I needed: a cast of anonymous, very friendly and weird—at times perhaps even intoxicated or homeless—characters, modern facilities, space, quiet, lots of resources, and a consistent atmosphere that I became increasingly familiar with. And that taught me what any good library does: it helps you work, gives you what you need, and makes you appreciate your community.

Housing Works Bookstore Cafe
126 Crosby Street

Housing Works is a charity that is not just famous for all the help it has provided to people affected by HIV/AIDS and homelessness for the past twenty-five years, but is also well known for being really good at something else: selling cool stuff. Housing Works has many different shops all around New York and Brooklyn, selling clothes and furniture, often very well curated according to the neighborhood and its inhabitants. Housing Works also hosts events—the bookstore is regularly (once a week sometimes) rented out for weddings—and online auctions.

The best part of the Housing Works empire, without a doubt, is its beautiful Bookstore Cafe on Crosby Street, right in the heart of SoHo. Many people sit there enjoying coffee or tea or even snacks and having a read. Other people, like myself, go in with their kids and leave them in the cute youngster section, while going off to either the rare section in the back behind the café, or the history, memoirs, and social sciences sections up on the mezzanine level. Often, I just enjoy having a stroll around the shop. The quality of the selection is so high you forget Housing Works is a thrift store at all—one day my sister even found a first edition of *Snoopy and the Red Baron* for a very reasonable price. I was quite jealous!

The great thing about shopping here is that not only is the selection rather excellent and very diverse, but you can buy in excess and guilt free; 100% of their profits go to fund Housing Works' lifesaving services, all of their stock is donated, and they are staffed almost entirely by volunteers. Above all, it's a really nice place to meet people or even just spend a pleasant Sunday afternoon reading books.

Mercer Street Books & Records
206 Mercer Street

Mercer Street Books & Records for me is an ultimate original New York destination. It instantly reminds me of my first few visits here—walking through SoHo and stopping for a minute to keep myself warm on winter days and having a quick little browse and buying a book I liked the cover of. For that very purpose, it is quite good that it is open until 10 p.m.—"or sometimes later," as is noted charmingly on the door.

If it ever disappears (though I hope that day never comes), I'll genuinely feel old. I don't think I've bought that much, nor do I visit too often, but I just love having it around and knowing it is there. It has that smell of dusty secondhand books that I love dearly. Everything in there, from the well-thumbed paperbacks to the racks of vinyl records, feels just the right amount of dirty, and the main man I've often seen working there fits right in—sort of friendly enough, but not at all intrusive, which is exactly what you want. Perfect for a secondhand bookshop.

I chose not to interview anybody in the shop, because I wanted to preserve some of the mystique of the place. I find it romantic and transcendental in its own way. The main information to bear in mind is that Mercer Street Books & Records has been where it is for the past twenty-five years, and loves and supports its historically literary neighborhood with the philosophy that "we are all writers within . . ." How nice. I hope the store and its familiarly comforting smell of books stays with us, supporting all writers and readers, for another quarter century at the very least.

Zachary on the corner of Mercer and West 4th Street

When I first went about the creation of this little book, there were all sorts of discussions involved. One of them was about what was going in and what was not. Something I was very keen on including were all the street vendors you can find on various corners of certain streets throughout the city. They offer wonderful classics in old paperback editions, which I usually prefer the look of over the newer printings, and random photography books or strange illustrated medium-sized books about folklore crafts or Japanese interiors or the different types of coral you can find in the sea. These books are often sold for six or seven dollars on the streets, instead of thirty or forty from a fancier or more "legit" fully operational bookshop. Personally, I love those street vendors. I am never certain if it is because of the bargains they offer or because they're so friendly and quirky—and I am known for not just engaging with, but also taking a serious liking to, an eccentric character.

One afternoon, on my way to Washington Square Park, I stopped by the stall on the southwest corner of the Mercer and West 4th Street intersection. Zachary, along with a rotating cast of three or four friends of his, was there. Friendly as ever, I asked him all the questions I had always wanted answers to. My main query was whether or not he minded if I included him in the book—as I didn't want to cause him any legal trouble—and he said he did not mind. I learned that books are a form of public expression, so one is allowed to set up wherever one wishes and to sell as many books as one wants right then and there, as a form of "freedom of speech." Per Zachary's advice, I then watched *BookWars* by Jason Rosette and *Sidewalk* by Barry Alexander Brown, which gave me a fuller insight into this world. I got to learn about all the people that used to sell so many more things on the street than they do now, and the constitutional right that allows them to sell books without any problem. I thought it was just glorious, and so special to be able to do that. It gave me yet again such faith, trust, admiration, and love for books—these magical little objects that bring so many people together.

Then there was something else that I really started to think about, which I had never realized. Zachary noticed my accent, and so he asked me if in London they also had street vendors like himself selling books. There are so many flea markets and "cool" authentic places to shop in London, like Portobello, but it dawned on me that the closest I had come to these street vendors were the kiosks along the Seine in Paris, which feel so touristy and not completely authentic in some cases. This may be the reason I am so obsessed by all these street vendors, who barely have tables and sometimes sell straight from the sidewalk itself: they are intrinsically "New York," and, as an expat, I just fell in love with that.

Zachary told me all of them used to have brick-and-mortar bookshops; one was in Iowa, and I started to imagine what life must be like there, and I got completely lost in my thoughts. I love getting lost, I love Zachary, I love the books I bought for only a few dollars. I cycled past him a few days later and waved; I hope I get to wave at him again many more times. You should go and see Zachary, and experience him for yourself.

Dashwood Books
33 Bond Street

My brother Alexis has very specific taste. And if there is one thing he is most specific about, it is books. He has very particular interests when it comes to those books, and he loves to indulge in that. He could spend hours or days, months or years, looking for a certain book that he will absolutely "need" to get his hands on—there was in fact an incident with a book he recently "needed" me to get from Dashwood, and when I didn't get it, it became a whole situation and there was some arguing and sulking involved. When I told him about this booklover's guide to New York, he really didn't care too much for it; but his only and immediate comment was: "Well, I hope you're putting Dashwood Books in there. It's the best bookshop in the world."

Of course, I had certainly intended to include Dashwood Books on this literary journey through New York—it is possibly the most preeminent destination for any sort of culturally or artistically trendy person who knows anything about anything—but until then, I had not quite understood the impact the shop had on people's lives. I suddenly realized how much a statement like that meant, coming from my rather quiet and sometimes unenthusiastic brother.

Yes, Dashwood Books is most definitely a Downtown pit stop if you intend to wander around NoHo, perusing and shopping for interesting things. And yes, it is the number one venue for a photography book signing or party of sorts, if you number among the top ten "coolest" people in the world. (I came to a David Sims signing for his Supreme book here once, and the line was so long I instantly gave up on even trying to buy it.) And yes, it is a masterfully and brilliantly curated little piece of modern history for any fan of aesthetically distinct and very niche photo books.

If you had to (and really only if you had to) compare Dashwood Books to anything in the world, it would almost be like a mixture of one of those specialized underground Tokyo scenester secrets and a Downtown hub where you can casually run into the person with the most street cred you'll ever encounter in a lifetime—like Rihanna, if you're so lucky. To get to the bottom of this and unveil all secrets, it was time to ask David Strettell (the genius behind the legend that is Dashwood) a few questions.

David Strettell
Owner of Dashwood Books

What prompted you to open Dashwood Books?
I wanted to run my own business and contribute to a medium I had a passion for.

What is the most expensive book you carry? What is the rarest book you have ever stocked?
Robert Frank's *Flower Is*—a book produced in Japan in an edition of only five hundred copies. I recently sold one for seven thousand dollars. Super-high production quality. I carry artists' books that can be simple homemade zines produced in editions of ten to fifty copies each—not particularly valuable in monetary terms, but a lot of love goes into them.

What's the go-to book you recommend your customers give someone as a gift?
Depends. I usually ask a few prying questions. But reliable starters in the photo-books world would be *William Eggleston's Guide*, Robert Frank's *The Americans*, and, for those looking for something a little more unexpected, Rinko Kawauchi's *Utatane*.

What are the greatest pleasures of owning a bookshop, and what is the most gratifying part of your job?
It's a lovely way of engaging with people. You find yourself building up a tremendous knowledge of a really narrow subject, and imparting that to other people is really gratifying . . . I always fancied myself as one of those "experts" on the *Antiques Road Show*.

Who is the most famous customer you have ever had in your shop?
Sam Shepard came in once during a signing event we had for Bruce Weber—he was the best-looking dude I've ever seen. And Rihanna came in once, too—she stood by the door and took her shades off slowly, saying, "Do you have anything for . . . me . . . ?"

What is the weirdest question you have ever been asked in the shop?
I have a strict dealer discount policy and most dealers respect it, but I had one guy who called up once after I refused to give him a better price on a rare book and pretended to be a rich Chinese businessman using a really bad fake Chinese accent to try and get a better discount.

You recently got into publishing. What drew you to that? Has it gone according to plan, and worked out the way you wanted it to?
Pretty much. Actually, we've been publishing for nearly a decade now. It takes up more and more of my time, but I think having access to artists helps promote the store, and it's helped me appreciate the medium even more.

What is the greatest enemy of the publishing world?
Bad books. There's a lot of crap out there.

How do you envision the future of bookshops?
For right now it seems pretty healthy—there seems to be more and more interest in publishing and books. Don't get me wrong: nobody's going to get rich running a bookstore, but it's definitely rewarding. I based my initial interest in bookstores on a Japanese model after a trip there about fifteen years ago. There were a few bookstores that carried unusual, beautifully crafted books from small publishers all over the world. The model for publishing came from the Köln-based bookstore Walther Koenig that began collaborating in the 1980s with artists like Hans-Peter Feldmann, Gerhard Richter, Boris Mikhailov, and Wolfgang Tillmans. I think keeping things in-house, produced on a small-scale to control the quality, is where it's at, and using the internet for this kind of product can be really useful—using the bookstore as a showroom.

If you wrote a book, where in New York would you set it? What street would the main character live on?
I always wondered what living in those mews near Washington Square Park would be like.

Where's the best place to sit down and read in New York?
Tompkins Square Park.

Aside from yours, what is the best bookshop in the city?
The Strand.

If you had to bring only one book with you to a desert island, which would it be?
The Idiot.

According to you, what's the best way to enjoy reading a good book?
Lying down on a beach—no music.

Strand
828 Broadway

If by any chance you are rifling through this book in the geographical order the pages are in, you have probably not yet been faced with the undeniable fact that everybody has answered that their favorite place to get books in New York is the Strand.

It's my favorite place, it's my sister (book-obsessed woman, inventor of the embroidered "book clutch") Olympia's favorite place, it's David Strettell's favorite place, it's where Denzel (Washington, that is) gets his books, and it was Michael Jackson's favorite place—or at least, he liked it enough to have it shut down so he could have the whole place to himself and his children (twice). It is the favorite place of anybody who lives or spends any time in New York, and it is the favorite place of any non–New Yorker on a visit here. If you would like to know why, the answer is very simple and can be summed up in three main points:

1 It has absolutely everything you need as far as books go, covering each and every topic imaginable. Not only that, the topics are covered in the most beautiful way, with books of extraordinary quality. The shop offers extensive variety in the choice of those books: new releases, secondhand books for a bargain, a whole floor dedicated to rare books worth a certain amount of money (but not always, there are also bargains up there!), signed editions (sometimes inadvertently mixed in with unsigned copies), a lovely kids' section, an amazing selection of arts, fashion, journalism, history, photography, erotica, architecture . . . Anything you need, you will find at the Strand. They have cool bookmarks, cards, and tote bags—good-quality, thick ones, if I may add: my sister brought me back a navy blue one with the red logo when she was on her first visit to New York as an adult, and I used it through the entirety of my (very long) university years. Last but not least, they sell cute and funny gifts, such as Trump's (proportionate) hands in a box available at every register. (Side note, everything, with the exception of certain rare items, is reasonably and fairly priced.)

2 The atmosphere there is unbeatable. When you first walk in, you feel like you are entering the movie set of a quintessential charismatic New York bookshop that could be from almost any era. It feels timeless, and at the same time, it is historic. Then you are absorbed by all the books, whether you are in the fiction section on the ground floor, or the photography department or anything else upstairs. You can get lost in the kids' section, which is full of all the classics from your childhood and has all imaginable toys and fun things for lil'uns. And when you make your way up to the third floor for the rare books, you will be utterly in heaven. You will feel like you are in a secret section of a library, you will indulge in it, and you will never want to leave. Everything up there feels beyond precious, but there are actually a surprising number of affordable tomes if you can't splurge just yet.

3 The Strand is cared for with the most tender and adoring love. In its third generation of family ownership, the Strand is one of the last remnants of Book Row (which was right around the corner).

I sat with the delightful Nancy Bass, literature lover, innovator, creative genius, current owner of the Strand, and daughter of Fred Bass (son of the Strand's original founder, Benjamin Bass), who revolutionized the bookshop and brought it to the glorious haven it is today. She has been unofficially involved in the family business since birth, and officially since 1986.

Everybody whom I've asked about the best place to get a book in New York has answered the Strand. How does that make you feel, and why do you think that is?

Well, it makes me feel elevated, that is what we are here for—to be a literary center. It has been ninety-three years in the making. We used to be part of Book Row, and now it's in its third generation of owners. We have great stock, great prices, wonderful people working here who love books and want to share their feelings about books. We sell books at every price range, from our dollar carts to the rare section. We host lots of events with opportunities for everybody to meet great authors.

The bottom line, though, is that we love books and we have books for everybody and in every price range. Being in New York, which is an amazing cultural center, we have access to great estates and book collections and booklovers. That is how the Strand started with my grandfather—it was a passion-felt business.

What was the Strand's mission and goal when it first opened?

The Strand started on Book Row in 1927. It was originally one of forty-eight bookstores (our estate manager wrote a book about Book Row). They were in competition with one another, yet it was a destination.

If you go way back in time, the Village had cheap rents, it attracted a lot of people of culture, all the writers came here, all the publishers came here, Astor established his library where the Joseph Papp theater is (that was the original Astor Library). There was the Mercantile Library right off of Fourth Avenue. Then the book publishers came, and the printers came. The publishers would almost always have a bookstore underneath. Scribner's was here, Biblio and Tannen, then Barnes & Noble opened around here. Everybody seemed to be seated there, and then off of that were the secondhand bookstores, which made up Book Row. We are the last remnant from that time.

Was there a pivotal moment when things changed at the Strand, and when it went "big"
and became what it is today?

In 1953, when we were on Fourth Avenue, there were three bookstores across from the post office. The Stuyvesant family still owned that parcel of land. Descendants of Peter Stuyvesant were our landlords and they sold it to a developer to make apartment buildings. The bookshops got kicked out, and so a lot of them started closing down on Book Row.

The pivotal moment was when the bookstores moved from Fourth Avenue to Broadway, which is where we are located today. The rent was $125 a month on Fourth Avenue, but we had the opportunity to move to a location which was bigger and had more foot traffic on Broadway for $400. My grandfather said he wanted to stay in the catalogue business and it was too risky, but my dad said he wanted to have a store and that we wouldn't survive in the catalogue business. So that was really the pivotal thing. We first had a small part of the building and then ended up taking more and more as the bookstore got more and more successful. My dad always wanted to buy the building, but it was owned by a family of twelve or fourteen people, and it wasn't until 2011 that we were able to buy it.

How has the literary scene changed in New York City since the Strand has been around?
What were the events at the Strand like back in the day, and what are they like now?

When I started working here it was all used books, there was no internet, no computer system, there was a lot of browsing. People didn't know what they would find, it was the serendipity of coming here; we really only focused on getting great books, but we also wanted to focus on being reasonably priced. We would make it up in volume and we really focused on getting people in here. So it was a lot about the atmosphere.

We didn't have to organize the books: we would price them, and then put them right in front of the pricing desk on a new arrivals table, so that was the first place you would look. After a week, we would shelve them in the right section: philosophy, religion, and so on. The prices were penciled in, and I always thought they'd be so easy to erase. Nothing was computerized, there were no barcodes. If you said, "Do you have this book?" we would have to go to the section with the customers and look. A lot of people would come and search, some were book collectors, they would look for first editions, pop-up books, they would look for Matisse books. Usually, they were very knowledgeable.

Fast forward to today: there is much more travel in the world, people are looking for interesting experiences that they don't find elsewhere, there is a gluttony of the same types of stores everywhere. So there are a lot of people who come from out of town who have never experienced something like us. They are coming to see the store, like a destination.

So now we sell everything: new books, remainders, used books, rare books, paperbacks, many different types of books . . . And we also have a line of unique things that we think are fun, which people have enjoyed a lot. The focus is still on books, but the rest is nice. There is often a seriousness of going to a bookstore, so you need a lightness and it is a good punctuation to have gifty things.

What do you love doing the most at the Strand?

My favorite thing to do is think of new ideas that we can try out. I love how creative everybody is here. Back in the day, authors would come in and just do readings. Recently we have been doing some book speed-dating events, which people love. It's like normal speed-dating, but in our rare book room and only about books. Our team matches people according to their literary tastes. We have so many people who have met and even had kids from meeting at the Strand, whether they are customers or people who work here. I have people who write to me all the time telling their stories, it is so moving for me. Patti Smith used to work here, and so did her sister. She met her husband because of the Strand.

This year we had Hillary and Chelsea together for the first time at their book signing. Salman Rushdie was here, so was David Sedaris. We have had instances of authors we weren't able to accommodate because it gets too crowded (Bernie Sanders and Bill Clinton, for example), which is part of why we have expanded the rare book floor.

Who is the most famous person you have ever had here?

Michael Jackson was here at least twice, and we had to shut the whole store. My dad did it once, and I did the second time. Jackie Onassis also came by. Bill Clinton snuck in last month. Tom Hanks was recently spotted roaming around. Diane Keaton was here. Ben Stiller was in just a few weeks ago. Frank Ocean was, too. Oh, and Denzel Washington was in here putting together his whole library—we offered to help, but he knew exactly what he was doing.

Is there a secret section in the Strand, like the notorious ones in libraries?

I guess that would be the proof area, which is unique to us. It has all these paperback versions, uncorrected versions of reviewers' copies. Dad was the first person to get reviewer's copies and sell them. So, for example, you would buy a $25 book for $5 and then sell it at half price. People could get a brand-new book for about $10. There was a bit of controversy around whether it was ethical or not, but people in the publishing industry were so underpaid, this would help. Then it is also nice to think these books would have a second life. Also, the rare book room is intimidating to people, so we are putting a stairwell in because people think it is exclusive and expensive—but there are first editions for $20 and loads of accessible stuff up there.

Tell me about the most valuable book in the shop.

We sold a copy of Shakespeare's second folio for $100,000 in 2006. At the moment, in the rare book section, we have the 152nd printed copy of *Ulysses* illustrated by Matisse, and signed by both him and Joyce. The legend goes that Matisse, having not read *Ulysses*, mistakenly illustrated drawings meant for *The Odyssey* instead, and Joyce, infuriated, only signed 250 copies of the 1,500 that were made. Its price has fluctuated a bit, but it is now going for $45,000.

What is the best place to find a great book within the Strand?

The carts outside have loads of good stuff. I'm always complaining about why this or that is there. I hear stories of people who find signed copies and things we miss that are in the normal shelves. There was once a signed copy of Will and Ariel Durant's *The Story of Civilization*. We also find so many things in books, like pictures, money, postcards. There is actually a basket filled with photos and letters tied to the time—you can easily discover how much lunch was in the 1980s. It is like a time capsule. There was also once a collection of children's letters, poems, and drawings from an elementary school in Texas writing to kids in New York after 9/11. Such treasures are often just found.

What is the best place to enjoy a book or write in the Strand?

The four leather chairs in the rare section are nice. There is also "the crying bench" on the second floor, from *The Fault in our Stars*. Some people just sit on the floor in the fiction section, or in the back of science fiction.

When was the mileage last done?

It was originally eight miles in the 1970s, and then in 1997, George Will came up with that quote during the financial crisis, that "the only part of Manhattan worth saving was the Strand's eight miles of books." Then we added a floor and got art books, and we measured and it was twenty-three miles—but that number didn't sound good, so we settled on eighteen miles. The books are measured spine to spine, there are approximately 2.5 million of them.

What would be a go-to book recommendation for a lost customer?

E. B. White's *Here is New York* is a nice reflection of New York in the old days. I also love biographies. I put Mihaly Csikszentmihalyi's *Flow* out there as an inspiration of mine at the moment.

Alabaster Bookshop
122 Fourth Avenue

Alabaster Bookshop is the perfect neighborhood landmark. Situated on the west side of Fourth Avenue just north of the East Village right below Union Square, it is a pleasant place to pause and the last of the crowd of secondhand bookshops that once lined Book Row (right around the corner from the Strand's current location). It also has the bargain carriages outside, and I love that—who doesn't love a bargain?

Inside, there is a nicely sized selection of art, photography books, and some lovely older editions of fiction. I always prefer that, aesthetically and even ecologically: older books have a nicer feel to them and I like things that go around visiting all different types of homes. Being so close to the Strand, Alabaster does well to distinguish its modest space from the miles of books at its larger competitor nearby, with a more cautious buying policy and a more rarefied stock as a consequence. The few young men I've seen working there stay out of your business while you rummage through their eclectic selection, which can be nice, and there is a rather old-school feel to the place—not unlike visiting those studious little shops near the Pantheon in Paris, which makes me feel at home.

Cooper Square
& the *Village Voice*
36 Cooper Square

The *Village Voice*'s final resting place in the East Village (it moved to the Financial District briefly before its closure) looks out over the Great Hall, where Abraham Lincoln delivered his historic Cooper Union address. Founded in 1955, the *Voice* was not only the country's first alternative newsweekly, but the nation's most important, dedicated to covering and championing the arts, civil rights, and counterculture at large. For decades, the *Voice* graduated and enlisted a motley contingent of pioneering, provocative, and keenly intellectual journalists. Alumni included dogged muckrakers like Wayne Barrett as well as critics, columnists, and illustrators such as Nat Hentoff, Michael Musto, Lynn Yaeger, Lester Bangs, Henry Miller, E. E. Cummings, Sasha Frere-Jones, R. Crumb, and Matt Groening. Now shuttered, the *Voice* will forever be remembered for doing what a good city weekly should do: give the city's underdogs an unwavering and fearless voice through its immersive avant-garde coverage of everything New York, from underground nightlife to political and economic injustices.

If you wish to go and pay a symbolic visit to the *Voice*'s old stomping grounds on your literary pilgrimage, there is now a nice little square with some benches in front of Cooper Union. Extricate yourself from the bustle of the Bowery, look up to the *Village Voice* inscription on the façade, and imagine all the great writing that was done up there.

THE EAST VILLAGE

T

he East Village is synonymous with the Beat Generation, and the streets still reverberate with the names and words of the many authors who stalked them—Jack Kerouac, Allen Ginsberg, John Clellon Holmes, and William S. Burroughs, to name just a few. Decades later, the East Village is still very much a cultural cauldron—and its distinct place in New York's literary history is forever cemented by acting as a setting for scores of critically acclaimed books from Patti Smith's *Just Kids* to Lynne Tillman's *Weird Fucks*. Though very different from what it used to be, it is still a neighborhood full of life, students, bookshops, literary landmarks, and famous authors.

Ottendorfer Library
135 Second Avenue

When you stop going to libraries, you kind of forget what they are all about. Public libraries in a city like New York are a place where a neighborhood's community can find peace and quiet and books within the confines of a calm, inviting, safe space to read, study, or do whatever they please. Almost like a place of worship, but with books substituting religion. So that means that if the library is a small, local one, it reflects the neighborhood.

I had never explored the East Village libraries, and to be honest, I had kind of gotten out of the "library scene" I once considered myself a part of. When it comes to libraries, you immerse yourself deep into the scene: you test out certain libraries and certain neighborhoods, you go through a thorough sort of pick and choose phase. But then, once you have picked and chosen, you retract yourself from the scene and in your head, you have your go-to five or six libraries in each neighborhood you frequent, and that is that.

I decided the East Village was an acceptable place (and even quite a nice one), so I picked the Ottendorfer Library, which, on Second Avenue (between 9th Street and Saint Mark's), happened to be the closest one. I had walked by that strip maybe a hundred times in my life, yet I had never noticed a library there. But there it was: a beautiful nineteenth-century Queen Anne and neo-Italian mix landmark, ornamented by terra-cotta putti, which incidentally also happened to be the first free library ever opened in New York in 1884. I had no clue that I was in such a prestigious and exclusive piece of history until . . . well, until I discovered it. Except for the poor air-conditioning and awkward computer lab far down in the depths of the basement, there's a divine wooden staircase, friendly staff, an insanely beautiful arched wooden front door, and rows of fashionably antique iron shelves in the back.

East Village Books
99 Saint Mark's Place

I've always liked East Village Books on Saint Mark's. It has quite an old-school feel to it, and it definitely fits very well in its neighborhood. It is the ideal place to go hunting for a good bargain or a good read, or even just some company, from the suitably affable people who work there—perfectly appropriate for a bookshop of that nature.

The bookstore is also quite individualistic when it comes to how it operates. For example, I read on their website (which, as a side note, has lots of rather handy tips about books and book storage) that they would prefer you go in and chat with them and "teach" them something rather than have you buy something that you won't necessarily read. They'd also rather buy books from you than sell books to you, which made me wonder where they get their money from if they are constantly buying instead of selling to us. I like the whole vibe there, very true to itself. It is important to have your own voice when you are selling books; I have noticed everybody has their own style of bookselling, and it should be like that. You are selling people's stories, so it is only natural you have your own story too.

My story is that the people at East Village Books would not like me, because I never sell any of my books. I just lug them around from one life to another, even when I move countries. I love books so much, I find it difficult to part with them. I am going on a bit, but that is what happens when you get lost down the long and windy narrow corridors of East Village Books. It has that smell I like, too—the smell of old books, read and reread by all kinds of different people. Long live books and the stories of all the people who have held them!

Poetry Nights in the East Village

The Poetry Project at Saint Mark's Church-in-the-Bowery *131 East 10th Street*
Nuyorican Poets Cafe *236 East 3rd Street*
Bowery Poetry Club *308 Bowery*

Sometimes I think I do not understand poetry. As a teenager, there was some French poetry that I was obligated to read for my baccalaureate, and in the end I became a bit infatuated by it. I turned into a serious Baudelaire fan, and from there discovered Apollinaire's *Alcools*. I also knew some of Verlaine's and Mallarme's stuff, and read a lot of works by Michaux, Breton, and a few other people from the surrealist movement, but that was about it. I do wish I knew more and was more invested in it.

For anyone growing up in New York, however, poetry—its language, its power, and especially its sound—has been as vital a component of the city's identity as jazz, graffiti, or any of the other art forms that have colored the streetscapes for decades. From the Beats snapping fingers in cafés to the politically charged voices of Hispanic poets continuing the legacy of Clemente Soto Velez, poetry is woven into the cultural history of the city—and the East Village is still home to some of the best places to experience that first hand.

First, there is **The Poetry Project**, which has been going on for more than half a century. It seems to have built a wonderful little community for poets to rejoice and express themselves together. If you are not a poet, you can still of course attend their readings, which take place at the beautiful old episcopal church St. Mark's in-the-Bowery, which, despite its name, actually stands on Second Avenue. The Project also offers fellowships for emerging writers.

Then, there is the **Nuyorican Poets Cafe**. Almost in Alphabet City, it is a legendary institution and local favorite that has been around for more than forty years. As well as poetry readings and open-mic nights, the Nuyorican also hosts other surprises, such as comedy, music, and all sorts of performance arts. Allen Ginsberg, a longtime neighborhood resident, was known to have called the Cafe "the most integrated place on the planet."

To complete your Village poetry tour, the **Bowery Poetry Club** holds readings and salons on Sundays and Mondays in a multidisciplinary space that also hosts film screenings, literary workshops, and, amusingly, burlesque performances. This creates a tiny bit of confusion, but at least you have options for various styles of entertainment. Founded by Bob Holman in 2002, Bowery Poetry Club is run by Bowery Arts + Science, a non-profit organization, and after just fifteen years on the scene has been dubbed "a haven for verse in all its forms" by *New York Magazine*.

VorteXity Books
Southwest corner of Saint Mark's and Avenue A

On the southwest corner of Saint Mark's and Avenue A, right across the street from Tompkins Square Park, you might be lucky enough to encounter what I like to refer to as the "Book Table." Behind the Book Table stands Jen Fisher, a beautiful young woman with dark hair and a piercing pair of pale green eyes, who actually refers to the Table (recently marked as a New York landmark on Google Maps, may I add) as VorteXity Books. Whenever I see VorteXity there, I (probably very offensively) always ask her where she's been and insist on the fact that I have come by and not found her when I needed her.

The Book Table appears at least four days a week, from either the end of February or the beginning of March through at least November. Whenever I stop by, Jen and I get into deep conversations about what she has today on the Table and how impeccably displayed her books are. She usually tells me about a poet she has recently discovered and loves, and how they remind her of so and so, and where she got this or that. She always has great female authors whom I admire and cannot always find the works of with a nice cover—Marguerite Duras, for example, or Virginia Woolf. She only carries books she knows and loves. I got a great copy of *Despair* from her last time—she does always have Nabokovs with very cool covers.

She cannot lug the rest around, she says, and she cannot make what she doesn't know look as presentable and interesting as those authors or stories she enjoys. But if someone does tell her about something, she writes it down in a little notebook that sits on her Buick with a can of Canada Dry, and takes notes for future reference. She will usually go home and look it up, and then study it to decide whether or not she likes it. "That's the great beauty of books, you see," she tells me. "You are always learning something, whether you appreciate it or not. And then sometimes, you will learn something which will change your view or your perspective on life forever."

If that Buick is her stockroom, then the sidewalk is her shop. She would never want a brick-and-mortar shop, even if someone just handed one to her. She prefers the street. But the Buick is what transports everything and does all the work. She has had to check a few times to make sure the books weren't too heavy—books are heavy, particularly when you are a petite woman, like her. She is the only woman in the sidewalk book-vending business. She travels around the country, looking for estate sales and old book collections. She enjoys that a lot, as well as every encounter she is fortunate enough to make through her job. She learns so much from it, and everybody helps her out. "That's what we are all here for, to help each other out, and if it can be done via books, then all the better. Books are magical little objects. Books are life changing."

One time, it was Patti Smith who helped her out: she invited Jen over to her house and signed loads of books so she could sell them for more money. Apparently, Patti used to also be in the book-vending business when she was young. This extremely literate and charming young woman does not just carry a beautifully curated Book Table; she also has quite a mesmerizing personality and a unique way of expressing herself. I left the Book Table slightly changed and enchanted; perhaps the books from VorteXity will change you, too.

McSorley's Old Ale House
15 East 7th Street

Established in 1854, McSorley's is the oldest continuously operated saloon in New York City. It has also been a gathering place for some of the city's most famous writers. There was a time when women were not allowed in McSorley's, and ale is not my favorite, so instead of giving you my account of this historical landmark, I thought it best to ask the legendary Geoff Bartholomew (poet and bartender for more than four decades) about what these sawdust-strewn floors have carried for the past century and a half.

In a city like New York that is constantly changing, how is McSorley's still standing after all these years?

McSorley's is still standing because the three owning families (McSorley, O'Connell/Kirwan, and Maher) own the building. The place would have disappeared long ago if there had been a commercial lease. Today's bars and restaurants rarely last more than ten or twenty years, as the landlord drives them out of business at their respective location by raising the rent to insane levels. McSorley's is also still there because its draw is that it hasn't changed much, if at all, over the 164 years it's been around. Generations of people continue to show up, linked by fathers and grandfathers, and mothers and grandmothers, and by having had memorable experiences at the bar, fun times and deep conversations.

What was it like living above the bar?

I lived above the bar for almost ten years, from 1970 to 1979. The building was crooked, which lent a physical charm to the planked floorboards and the horsehair plaster, which sometimes collapsed in ceiling spots. Living above the bar meant one was available for any shift, especially if somebody got sick, or a snowstorm prevented staff from getting into town. It was a small apartment—tub in the kitchen, which most of us would rig into a shower, a pull-chain flush toilet (most have been replaced since then), a couple of rooms with no windows. Earlier in the nineteenth century, the apartments were actually used as a rooming house, as tenants would literally rent rooms, and this practice has once again surfaced in today's rental market since space is at a premium all over the city. Characters who've lived above the bar include Dan Lynch and his mom, who had fought in the Easter Rising in 1916; Bob Bolles, a local painter and sculptor; Doc Zory, a gypsy violinist; and Otto Arnold, a former bar chef, who died in 1980 but is shown in a photo on the wall throwing down the sawdust in 1940.

How many authors do you think have drunk at McSorley's? What attracted them to the place? Who was the most famous?

Joe Mitchell was probably the most famous author to frequent McSorley's. He was a regular, in and out of the bar in the 1940s through the 1970s. He would nurse a couple of ales at the second table on the left, which is the one he preferred, especially in the early afternoon when the sunlight poured in, bathing the tables. Paul Blackburn, the poet, was a regular in the 1950s and 1960s and lived next door toward the end of his life. I would run into him in the hall upstairs as he was using Bob Bolles's apartment to write in, since it afforded him a quiet place to work. Unfortunately, he had throat cancer from the Pall Malls he chain-smoked, and I think it was 1971 when he died. Other frequent writers were the composers Harrigan and Hart back in the 1870s and 1880s; then George M. Cohan, the Broadway producer and songwriter, from 1915 through the 1930s; Reuel Denney, the poet; E. E. Cummings in the 1950s; and maybe the most recently famous author, Frank McCourt. Numerous authors and playwrights have stopped by, as well as famous cinema actors and actresses, and still do so today. All these guys were attracted to the bar by their artist friends, painters, writers, poets, or actors. It was an easy place to sit down and have a few ales and talk and brainstorm their latest works or relationships. Same goes on today.

Do you think the fact that you and your son Rafe Bartholomew (who wrote a book about the bar called **Two and Two: McSorley's, My Dad, and Me***) became authors is related to your connection with McSorley's?*

I don't think Rafe or I became writers because of the bar. It obviously has provided material, but Rafe's writing career began in high school as a humor columnist, and I began writing short stories and poems when in the Peace Corps in Paraguay in 1968 or 1969, and continued to develop as a writer after I moved above the bar in 1970.

Do you feel honored and privileged to have worked and been around such an institution as McSorley's, or was it all just a day-to-day grind?

It is definitely a privilege to have worked in such a famous bar, the oldest continuing bar in New York. And yes, at times it could be a grind, especially if you had to work eight or nine or ten days in a row. I became part of the family, so to speak, as did most of the regular guys, all of us staying twenty years and more before moving on due to marriage or death or career changes. Lots of longevity and camaraderie at McSorley's.

Tell me about your writing endeavors and processes.

Poems: Write down first drafts. Then rewrite. Rewrite again. Read aloud, rewrite again. Read aloud. Rewrite. Do this a dozen times, sometimes twenty. Sounds excessive, but it's not. And even after the poem is in print you end up wanting to change a word here or there.

What are some of the literary anecdotes you can tell me in connection to the bar?

As I mentioned earlier, Joe Mitchell would drop by in mid-afternoon or early evening on an off night; he wasn't that fond of crowds. He would come in dressed in his gray suit and a black fedora, come up to the bar and order a couple of ales, then go sit down at that second table, assuming nobody else was at it. I remember one night in the late 1970s, it was a dead night so I let the sidekick bartender take over and I went and sat down with Mitchell and asked him what he thought of all the change in the city. He said it was inevitable that the city would change, he had seen it happen all his life, the city characters of the mom-and-pop stores and the marginal disappear, that we were all products of our time, of our generation. It didn't come out as negative, but you could tell by his tone that he was weary, worn out.

Then, out of the blue, he said his wife was ill, it was bad, and that McSorley's was one of the few places where he could go and sit and be alone and listen to himself think. I shared with him about my mom, who had been bedridden since 1972 with a horrific stroke, and he said that Therese, his wife, had been stricken as well. Just a bizarre coincidence. We talked more about the changing city, but I can't remember any specifics. It just seemed like everyone had become much more materialistic, I think that's what his line of thinking was. Not much different from today's change, except today is the explosion of building growth and exponential increases in the cost of city living. Mom-and-pop stores closing everywhere, dead storefronts in much of the West Village now as well.

Another time, in 1973, Joseph Heller came in with Kurt Vonnegut. They stood at the bar and had a couple of lights and a couple of darks and laughed a lot for about ten minutes straight. I wasn't working that shift, but happened to be grabbing a free meal in the back room and recognized them both because I was working on an M. A. in Creative Writing at City College, and both Heller and Vonnegut were teaching there at the time (I had Vonnegut for the year-long seminar between 1973 and 1974). I was too insecure to go engage them, and rightly so. To just see these two great writers hanging out and laughing so hard was a visual treat I can still see in my mind. And a couple of times in the 1970s, Woody Allen would come in his green army fatigue jacket, have a couple of ales, then leave. Nobody ever seemed to recognize him, though he was known to frequent village joints in that particular outfit.

What to you is the most interesting piece of history associated with the bar?

My favorite artifact is the pair of ankle irons hanging from the ceiling next to a bullwhip mid-bar. They were brought back by an Irishman, who fought for the Union and was captured and imprisoned at Andersonville, the horrible Civil War prison of the Confederates, and a friend of John McSorley, who hung them up behind the bar. The signed photo of Babe Ruth's farewell ("The Babe Bows Out")—Nat Fein won a 1948 Pulitzer Prize for this photo, I think—at old Yankee Stadium in June of 1948 is always a poignant thing to look at for me. I wrote a poem about it, and still think it's one of my best.

Back in the day, was the bar a real hotspot in the literary scene of New York? Do you think it still is?

McSorley's was a literary hangout from 1915 to 1935, the era of Eugene O'Neill, George Jean Nathan the critic, some painters, notably Bellows, and specifically John Sloan, who painted McSorley's four or five times, all of them famous now. There were others in that group as well, but names escape me now. In the late 1950s and 1960s, poets and writers hung out here—Gil Sorrentino, Joe Flaherty, Paul Blackburn, the painter Jim Johnson, de Kooning was part of this group, many of them going back and forth between McSorley's and the Cedar Tavern on University Place. De Kooning liked McSorley's because he was at one time a neighbor of the O'Connells, who owned the place. Actually, Dorothy O'Connell owned the place from 1938 to 1974, died, and then her husband Harry Kirwan ran it until 1977, when he sold it to Matt Maher, the current owner.

Stanley Crouch, the columnist and jazz author and critic, used to come in and relax in the back, as well as Hettie Jones, the wife of LeRoi Jones. Nowadays, one of the greatest American novelists alive, James McBride, comes in on Fridays for a seltzer and a chili, and brings his whole writing class from NYU in to check out the place for lunch. The book jacket of *The Good Lord Bird* is on the wall.

Do you think any books have actually been written in the bar? What would be the inspiration for writing in the bar?
Probably some books or pieces of books have been written in the bar. There are whole panels of comic books that have scenes set in McSorley's. So many things in the bar, historical and beautiful. The December 2013 cover of the *New Yorker* had McSorley's in the snow with Winnie the Pooh going inside—great cover. Then you could go look at an original invitation to the Brooklyn Bridge on the wall, or an 1880s playbill for a vaudeville show titled McSorley's Inflation by Harrigan and Hart. Also a photo of the duo of vaudeville composers sits behind the bar, next to a signed letter from Franklin D. Roosevelt. A pair of handcuffs Houdini got out of in 1904 are hanging above the old icebox, which itself dates to 1835, pre-McSorley. All kinds of goodies.

What have been your best or most gratifying moments working at the bar or writing a book about the bar? And the most challenging parts of either of those?
Writing the two volumes of *The McSorley Poems* has probably been most satisfying to me, because I was able to capture and express some of the significance and passion and poignancy of the physical place and the characters who work and pass time at the bar.

What is your favorite place to buy or borrow a book in New York? And the best place to read or write in the city?
Best place to buy a book is the Strand—hands down the best, and a survivor in its own right. Best place to read in New York is on the Hudson River Walkway below 14th Street, all the way down to the Battery. Great walking, reading, biking, running along the path, great pocket parks along the way, and the river flowing, always flowing. My late wife would rise at 6 a.m., rollerblade down to the end of the island and back, five days a week. Best place to write is in your apartment in the morning, at night, whenever you can steal time and bribe your muse.

If you had to repaint the bar in a fun and extravagant color, what would it be?
I'd paint the ceiling a Patriot Red, because it would age well, turning into a burgundy over time, and would set off all the artifacts that fill the walls.

Mast Books
72 Avenue A

One of the first bookshops that I became very attached to in New York was Mast Books on Avenue A. A friend introduced me to this amazing little shop when I was writing a "City Guide to New York" for a French magazine about a decade ago. I was quickly drawn to its broad selection of secondhand books, which was quite diverse but still very meticulously curated.

Nothing they sell here is of poor taste or quality, and the shop has none of that sort of "dirty secondhand" feeling whatsoever—no judgment there, I do love rummaging through dusty relics; but an occasional break from that can be refreshing. Having moved to a new corner location (still on Avenue A) in 2018, the shop feels clean, airy, and "feng shui" approved. The display tables and shelves are arranged in a very modern way and there is a sort of "designed" aspect to the whole place, which perfectly reflects some of the books on sale.

What I love the most about Mast is that you always feel like you are discovering some sort of treasure—whether it's a hidden gem you've only ever seen for sale there, or a limited-edition photo book you've been in search of for years—and the price is surprisingly always right. It feels like the owners (a married couple) don't believe in ripping off their customers or taking advantage of them and cashing in on their knowledge and expertise in the field, which I find is a generous and inviting approach to selling rare and valuable books. With these very fair and competitive prices, not only do you feel like you are getting a great deal, but it also restores your faith in the idea that brick-and-mortar is not dead yet. Mast Books is a great place to find someone an original and thoughtful gift, especially if that someone is you.

Karma Bookstore
136 East 3rd Street

Brendan Dugan is a fixture in the contemporary art scene, hosting rather famous artists' shows, book signings (Rob Pruitt was seen scribbling on *Pattern and Degradation* volumes in the nude at a former West Village location), and special events at a rotation of various addresses. His most recent endeavor, though, was the opening of a refreshing and modern bookshop called Karma Bookstore, which is directly affiliated with—and only one block behind—Dugan's gallery of the same name.

The gallery's bookshop was getting too full, so Dugan was in desperate need of more space. The shop, which incidentally was previously the location of the long-admired and beloved St. Mark's Bookshop (R.I.P.), had been vacant for a while; given how close it was to the gallery, it seemed made to be.

The shop sells all sorts of sophisticated and rare art books, as well as the expected selection of exhibition catalogs and artists' books. It has a few kids' things to the side of some shelves, too. The gallery also publishes some of its own books, so it does offer quite a charming medley.

(Only two blocks away from the well-respected Mast, you may consider going on a little fashionable arty book tour of the area.)

Bonnie Slotnick Cookbooks
28 East 2nd Street

I remember my sister stumbling upon a deliciously decorated cavern full of countless cookbooks many years ago and being absolutely mesmerized. As soon as I started my book pilgrimage, she immediately evoked the delightful shop, located in an old West Village tenement first-floor apartment, where we had spent a whole afternoon snooping around—once home to all sorts of antique cooking utensils, oddities, and out-of-print cookbooks—wondering if it was still there. I spent another whole afternoon on a Citi Bike trying to locate the superb gem we remembered so fondly. I also endangered myself for most of the ride sending my sister photos of random West Village first floors, before going home disappointed. A few days later, my sister sent me an old photo she had of the shop, and we quickly found out it was called Bonnie Slotnick.

When I paid a visit to Slotnick's new location (three times the size of the previous one) along one of the more charming streets of the East Village, I told her that long and boring story. I was holding my phone in one of my hands. She pointed to it and said, "I don't have that object, but even I know you can just type 'cookbook shop New York' in Google and find me." It was weird, but that had never even crossed my mind—Slotnick's previous little shop felt so personal and intimate that I thought it was almost like a secret living room society, something very far removed from that very public space called the internet.

Slotnick's new shop, which she moved into in 2015, is much bigger, but still preserves the same qualities of her old West Village place: intimate, unique, cozy, beloved, and deeply cared for. She was dog-sitting Goldie when I stopped by, and fussing over what I thought was an already beautifully arranged display of shelves. She brought over those shelves from the West Village, chopped the tops off, and used them to cover the rest of the square footage of her new locale.

The selection is as exquisite as all her little decorative trinkets, with everything from brand-new cookbooks from the trendiest restaurants to obscure nineteenth-century epicurean references; and the ambiance has something of a comforting country kitchen you would want to snuggle up in, whilst surrounded by the smell of freshly baked cakes.

We discussed the lovely signage outside (thanks to which you will not miss this incarnation of the store), and she expressed how lucky and grateful she felt for her new landlords, who are so much more generous and understanding than the West Village ones. They gave her a suitably long lease, which means that, thankfully for us, we will be able to visit this wonder for many more years to come. There is even a garden in the back that visitors can take advantage of during weekdays. It was sort of late on a Saturday evening, and Slotnick was closing, but I felt as if I could have spent the night there. I left enchanted and thrilled—so happy about all the bookshops I have had the pleasure of seeing on this journey and the people I get to go and bother.

Codex
1 Bleecker Street

The opening of Codex (the Latin for handwritten manuscript in book form) in early 2018 restored my faith in the bookselling industry. Discreetly connected to Think Coffee, Codex is a cute corridor-like shop right off the Bowery, at the very beginning of Bleecker Street. I liked its physical connection to Think very much, not only because the coffee shop is somewhat dear to me (a daily local of mine, where cups are compostable and staff is friendly), but because that vibe of a laid-back secondhand book-shop attached to a coffee shop is something I find quite special. It almost feels like you are on a film set in New York, and the bookshop person and the coffee person are going to fall in love, or people will meet in each respective place and then flirt, and then maybe marry at the end of the rom-com. I love that.

Leaving aside that fantasy, Codex feels intimate, a little tight (very crowded the times I was there, which is a good sign), and has an overwhelmingly pleasant atmosphere. Secondhand books of all sorts—from literary fiction to cool rare art books—fill the room, precious tomes are stacked all the way to the top of the shelves, and there's a small table of new books right beside the connecting door to the coffee shop. I found out the table belonged to someone who used to sell books on the street, which only made me like the place even more.

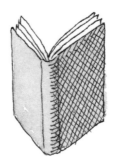

THE WEST VILLAGE & GREENWICH VILLAGE

Washington Square

Situated side by side like close siblings, the West Village and Greenwich Village have long been favorite neighborhoods for many esteemed New Yorkers. Both have their own distinct personalities; the former a bit more insulated and moneyed, the latter more academic and bohemian. Together they are notable for not only their cultural wealth and historical diversity, but also for being home to scores of important literary and artistic figures throughout the years. Today, this corner of the city remains an enclave for some of the city's most influential personalities, whether they are famous and glitzy celebrities or underground intellectuals.

The area is not just fertile ground for literary luminaries, it is also a pleasant, and green refuge, with a mysterious old-school charm that is second to none. Take a stroll, indulge, and keep an eye out for those informative red historical plaques to discover which of your preferred authors resided in the beautiful secluded townhouse down that secret alley you just stumbled upon!

Residence of Willa Cather
& Richard Wright
82 Washington Place

Washington Square Park (and the streets surrounding it, including and especially University Place) is and always has been my favorite area in all of New York. But this is not about one's love and obsession for a park with a dog run and a playground, nor is it about the various forms of juggling or music or dancing or skating around the fountain; this is about a nostalgic stroll down memory lane and a quest for history-filled, beautiful old homes of some of our literary heroes.

Oh, to picture Willa Cather, author of *My Ántonia*—incidentally, a favorite of Joanne Hendricks, the owner of Cookbooks—writing her first novel, *Alexander's Bridge* (1912), up in one of the apartments of this gorgeous Greenwich Village beige brick gem. And to top it off, Richard Wright is said to have written his autobiography *Black Boy* in there too, in 1945.

Minetta Tavern
113 MacDougal Street

I first heard the words "Minetta Tavern" when I was watching an episode of *Mad Men* and Peggy was meeting some of the boys there. Something of a New York institution, it has an Americanized classic French décor (and I am French, so I can say that), and a rather pleasant yet sometimes noisy atmosphere, and the strange power to lure you back without you really knowing why. When I moved to New York and found it was already in my husband's rotation, I began to acquire knowledge about Minetta Tavern's rich history, which only made me grow fonder of the place.

Minetta had a much different existence in the 1940s as a modest eatery and bar, which attracted struggling artists and writers. Known as The Black Rabbit until 1929, Minetta then re-opened in 1937, and counted the likes of Ernest Hemingway, E. E. Cummings, and Ezra Pound among its regulars. Later on, during the Beat Generation, Minetta is known to have been rented out for friends of William S. Burroughs, Lucien Carr, and Allen Ginsberg.

Today, Minetta can still be a magnet for the Downtown literati—and, I suspect, for those like me, who are homesick for French food, and enjoy it seasoned with a sprinkling of the city's literary history.

MacDougal Street
Where lots of literary things have happened

Step out of Minetta Tavern, cross over Minetta Lane and, at 115 MacDougal, you will find Café Wha?. If you wish to go on a bit of a Beat Generation tour, this is your opportunity to do so! In 1961, a nineteen-year-old Bob Dylan performed his first concert here. Many Beat Generation authors were in attendance, and Café Wha? is known to have been on Allen Ginsberg's regular circuit.

Another important note while touring MacDougal Street is that at number 130 (now part of NYU's Law School) lived Louisa May Alcott's uncle. She may or may not have written some of the last paragraphs of *Little Women* there. Whether or not this actually happened remains one of the unsolved mysteries of New York's literary past; but it is more interesting and appealing for everybody if we assume it did, so we shall leave it at that.

Hamish Bowles

International editor-at-large for *Vogue*, excellent writer, legendary fashion expert, notoriously obsessed by the color lilac, collector of beautiful clothes and marvelous books. Very sophisticated and fabulous English expat living in Greenwich Village for more than three decades

Hamish Bowles

You're a legend in the fashion world, a well-respected journalist, and a collector of clothes. How is your work and passion across fashion reflected in your library?

Extensively! I have a whole section dedicated to fashion monographs and related books—in fact, I have so many that I ran out of space, so they are now also stacked in wobbly book pyramids everywhere. There is also an ever-increasing area of the books that I have worked on—exhibition catalogues for *Jacqueline Kennedy: The White House Years*; *Balenciaga and Spain*; *House Style: Five Centuries of Fashion at Chatsworth*; and of course so many *Vogue* tomes that they practically form their own library.

What's the fashion bible or the most essential book in your opinion?

Cecil Beaton's *The Glass of Fashion* is an invaluable look at the tastemakers of the first half of the twentieth century, as is Bettina Ballard's *In My Fashion*. She was the fashion director of American *Vogue* in the 1950s and has amazing personal insights into the worlds of culture, fashion, and society from the 1930s to the 1950s.

What type of books do you read for work? What do you read for pleasure? And how do they differ?

I have wildly eclectic reading tastes. I enjoy biographies—recently adored Bill Cunningham's memoir *Fashion Climbing*, and Count Kessler's *Journey to the Abyss*. I'm on an André Aciman jag at the moment, having so relished *Call Me By Your Name* and *Out of Egypt*. I sometimes revisit the classics that I read so voraciously as a teenager. And, a lot of fashion, style, society autobiographies, and monographs for research.

If you wrote a book of fiction, where would you set it in New York? In Greenwich Village? And what street would the main character live on?

Well, it would be set between New York and Tangier. Washington Square Park and Harlem, 125th Street.

Where is the best place to acquire (buy, borrow, or find) a book in New York?
Three Lives & Co. at 154 West 10th Street—a valiant last standout from the fast encroach
of fashion boutiques. Jane Stubbs always has fabulous historic style books, as well as related
works on paper—now at KRB, at 138 East 74th Street.

Where do you like to read or write?
At home, propped up in bed on flowering Porthault sheets in my lilac cretonne bower, or
propped up with lilac chintz and purple Fez embroidery cushions on my marmalade velvet
tufted sofa.

*How have the fashion scene and the literary scene changed since you first moved
to New York?*
Fashion has changed beyond all recognition, because the internet and the world of commu-
nication that we now inhabit has opened it up to all in the most democratic way. When I first
came to New York in the 1980s, there was much more sleuthing involved—you had to do
your research on the ground to discover who was new and exciting and how you could possibly get into their shows or find their work. The literary world seems less changed, although
of course technology has transformed the way we communicate ideas and devour them.

*What's the most precious (in rarity, or monetary or sentimental value) book that
you've ever been in possession of?*
I'm delighted to own Carlos de Beistegui's copy of the album produced for the Duke and
Duchess of Devonshire's Costume Ball that celebrated Queen Victoria's Diamond Jubilee.
It was a presentation volume that was given to the guests who sat in their costumes for the
fashionable photographers and portraitists of the day. Of course I was much absorbed with
research into this when I curated *House Style* at Chatsworth last year, and of course the prov-
enance is wonderful as de Beistegui was such a legendary host himself.

What would be the most fashionable way to enjoy a good book?
Waiting for the Vetements show to start, or ideally in the hour and a half it takes to get to
the show from central Paris.

What book would you bring on your next fashion tour?
I'm loving André Aciman's books and I'm certainly relishing Tina Brown's *Vanity Fair Diaries*
. . . and I've brought *A Little Life* by Hanya Yanagihara on about thirty trips—hopefully one
day I'll find the time to actually read it.

*We all know you love lilac, but what would be the most hideous color to paint
bookshelves or a library?*
White.

Jefferson Market Library
425 Avenue of the Americas (Sixth Avenue)

When I walked around the West Village as a tourist, I would often just take photos of this magnificent, rather official looking Victorian Gothic–style architectural gem. I was never quite sure what it was, but it constantly popped up, rain or shine, and always stood out in my random photos of the lower Village New York skyline, among the big overarching traffic lights, and what was a relatively modern and conventional-looking row of buildings. Yet there it always was: the Jefferson Market Library, originally built in 1875 for a steep $360,000. Voted one of the ten most beautiful buildings in America by a poll of architects in the 1880s, it also housed a police court on the first floor (now the Children's Room), a civil court on the second floor (now the Adult Reading Room), and a holding area for prisoners on their way to trial or jail (now a quiet brick-arched Reference Room in the basement).

Fast-forward to my library-obsessed New Yorker life: I was spending my days two levels below ground at the Mulberry Street branch of the NYPL. One day, out of the blue, my friend Dineen said, "I don't understand why you don't just use the library near my place in the West Village." I realized she was talking about the Jefferson Market Library, and following that day, I never really returned (until very recently, as a pilgrimage) to the subterranean location I had so much affection for on Jersey Street.

The Jefferson Market Library is an absolutely perfect library. It has everything one could need (except a lavatory!). The atmosphere is delightful for writing or studying—quiet as a church. The building is beyond exquisite. The staff is near to invisible, which I cherish. The crowd is a mixture of real students (unlike myself), charismatic locals, and quite a heavy population of older people, whom I always find are perfect library goers because they usually know what they are looking for, find it quickly, and then sit down and read it—or else borrow it and go home.

Library

Unoppressive Non-Imperialist Bargain Books
34 Carmine Street

I am not sure how or why (especially with a name like that), but one often forgets about this unforgettable and remarkable literary enclave. Unoppressive Non-Imperialist Bargain Books is discreetly located on one of the more pleasant, less crowded streets of the West Village—Carmine Street sort of sits to the side, with its wide and airy pavements, offering a much calmer stroll than its busier neighbor, Bleecker.

Established more than a quarter century ago, this unique and personal bargain-book paradise was recommended by the *Village Voice* for anyone "with writer's block or boredom or suffering from a complete lack of cash." As I fluctuate between having all of those and having none of those, it seems almost the perfect place for me on my lonely days. Down its long corridor of secondhand and very cheap books, you will find whatever you need or did not know you needed in a charismatic shop full of spirit and grit. It has also served as a political safe house many a time—it was one of the four Manhattan headquarters for the Bernie Sanders campaign in 2016, and in 2011 it housed the Occupy Wall Street library for a short while. Stop by and say hello to Jim Dougras, the friendly owner who, with his long white hair and Stetson, you will not miss.

Another interesting little fact about this place is its "lodgers." Unoppressive also houses a comic shop (manned by a friendly young lad who also speaks French, and will fill in for Dougras on the off chance he is not there), and a sort of strange law, finance, or tax literature stall in the back, the purpose of which I did not fully understand. The comic books man also told me that there used to be a miniature cellphone shop in the window, too. All of those fun facts only made Unoppressive even more unorthodox and lovable than it already was.

bookbook
266 Bleecker Street

Originally located on the corner of Bleecker and West 11th (now Bookmarc), bookbook used to be called the Biography Bookshop and was a West Village favorite for locals as well as visitors. A worthy successor to the space, bookbook's current location features special discounts on brand-new books, and a selection that is usually top-notch, especially for kiddies!

The smallish but comfortable bookshop has a uniquely local feel to it, and reminds me of certain discount shops I used to go to a lot in London—there was one right in front of Notting Hill Gate tube station, where you could get amazing and really fun kids' books for a couple of pounds or so. There is also something genuine about bookbook, with its quirky staff and a serene and soothing atmosphere within the shop.

The books are new, the prices are low, the selection is eclectic, and there is a bit of everything for everybody: the perfect children's selection, cool New York books if you are on a special visit and need to bring something back, the latest novels if you want to be in the mix, and old classics if you need to do some catching up. But what I like the most at bookbook are the people who work there. They mind their own business (which I like, because I need my freedom and independence when I shop—especially for books), but at the same time they are super helpful and attentive when called upon. They will find anything you need, they will wrap anything you buy, and they will do most of it with a smile and sometimes a joke, if you are lucky. And unless it is raining, there is always a table of stuff outside (books, notebooks, or postcards, perhaps?) to draw you into the shop.

Three Lives & Company
154 West 10th Street

An undeniable favorite of not just every local, but also any Village goer or walker, is Three Lives & Company. Established in 1978 (it was in another West Village location for five years, before moving to its current one in 1983), this quaint corner shop has also been baptized "one of the greatest bookstores on the face of the Earth" by Michael Cunningham, who most definitely knows what he is talking about, as he happens to be a Pulitzer Prize–winner for Fiction.

With its divine location and look, Three Lives & Company is a neighborhood staple where you can find any of the new releases, classic fiction, nonfiction, art, or photography books all perfectly displayed along its neatly organized shelves. Three Lives & Company is not just a pleasant local hangout, it is a testament to the West Village's lovely and loving atmosphere. This would be one of the more appropriate places to visit in the neighborhood if you were after some summer reads recommendations, as the staff is knowledgeable and famous for "reading prodigiously."

Bookmarc
400 Bleecker Street

There was something undeniably exciting about Bookmarc when it first opened. The über-cool and very trendy fashion powerhouse that increasingly seemed to be the only tenant of Bleecker Street was branching out. After baby clothes, younger people clothes, gadgets and gifts (mostly to be found at Marc by Marc Jacobs), clothes for men, shoes for feet, and anything for any body part or for any taste, gender, or age, Marc Jacobs was now offering books for eyes and minds. Not only that, the books are awesome.

Bookmarc is absolute perfection in terms of finding a gift for anybody you like or love, or treating yourself to something exquisite that you never knew you needed. Bookmarc is also ideal for discovering hidden treasures— whether it's random vintage finds mixed into the shelves with our favorite literary classics (usually adorned with nicer covers than in other shops), or a graphic design book on all the different typefaces in existence, or a unique signed edition of a photography book you'd never seen before, or some really rare imports from Japan or any en vogue international destination. The selection at Bookmarc is somewhere between intellectual, highly fashionable (of course), sophisticated, culturally diverse, and really enjoyable.

Also, let's not overlook how incredibly refreshing and "Zen" the design of the store is, which not only makes it fun to hang out there (or attend book signings, which they regularly host), but also makes every item you purchase from there look inevitably impressive. Oh! And did I mention they moved over a lot of the cute trinkets from Marc by Marc Jacobs? So you can still buy that lipstick pen and one of the best notebooks in the biz over there. And, last but not least, none of us will ever look as cool as the people who work there; but that's okay, because despite how fabulous and intimidating they look, they're still really friendly.

Bookshop

Marc Jacobs

New York born and bred fashion designer, booklover, and owner of Bookmarc

Marc Jacobs

Tell me about your personal book collection. What is the most valuable book in there?

When I lived in Paris I had a proper library, which was really a big room with lots of bookshelves. I've always been a booklover and I love to read when I'm on vacation or when I can find time. I especially love research books, art books, and printed matter such as zines from the 1980s. Anytime I'd go see an exhibition or anything art-related, I was usually with John Reinhold, who's a great art collector. He introduced me to lots of art, and we would buy the catalogue from each show we went to see. We couldn't buy it for ourselves, we had to buy it for each other, and we'd write to each other how we felt about that day, how we felt about the show. So on a sentimental level, all my books I bought with John Reinhold from exhibitions, galleries, and shows that I saw are pretty valuable to me.

Then there are rare books, which are some of my favorite books. I have a couple of signed first editions by Joan Didion that I love, like *Slouching Towards Bethlehem* and *The White Album*. I also have some art books that are very rare—they're either out of print or limited editions. The first artworks I ever bought were prints by Mike Kelley. They were defaced pages from history books, like the kind of history books you would have in school, and he drew penises or tits on the images. Then in sync with this exhibition of prints, which were taken from those books, he also made a book of all those defaced pages called *Reconstructed History*, in only a very limited edition. That is one of my most valued books.

There are also books that were gifts from friends, which are obviously very sentimental. I have a lot of artist friends who have given me books, such as Rachel Feinstein, John Currin, or Elizabeth Peyton, so any of those, which have a dedication to me or are from an artist are among my most prized and sentimental books.

What was your favorite book as a kid?

That would probably be *The Cat in the Hat* or *The Lorax* by Dr. Seuss. Dr. Seuss in general was my favorite children's book author. Maurice Sendak wrote one of my favorite children's books—*Where the Wild Things Are*. And I always loved reading the *Nutshell Library* by Maurice Sendak, with treasures like "Chicken Soup with Rice" and "Pierre" because of how tiny the books are and the stories themselves.

You are a born and bred New Yorker, and now you have Bookmarc. Is it fun to have your own bookshop in the city?

I love books and I love printed matter. I'm not super attached to electronics and modern-day ways of reading; I like to carry around magazines and books, and I like to keep books after I finish reading them and I prefer them in hard copies, and all that stuff. We saw there was a little bookstore in the West Village that was going out of business. It had always been there. When we moved Marc by Marc into the West Village, we made this commitment because so many people said there goes the neighborhood as they're opening a fashion store in the West Village. Robert [Duffy] and I wanted to contribute to the community. We love the West Village. We live in the West Village. I'm a New Yorker. So if anything, we wanted to contribute so we did various things in the store, like having a Santa and picture taking. When the bookstore on the corner became available, we decided to take it but keep it as a bookstore. Then, with the help and curating genius of Jen Baker, Bookmarc became this living, breathing, beautiful thing where we had events, authors signed books, we collected books, sold magazines, sold Olympia [Le-Tan]'s bags, and it felt like an extension of our personalities. Jen being a great knower of old New York from back in the day and still being connected to people in the art and music scene, it felt from the start like a tribute to all that was good about New York and giving back to a community rather than paving paradise to put up a parking lot sort of thing.

In your opinion, as a New Yorker, when might have been the most interesting time to run a bookshop in New York?
Oh, I don't know but I can imagine—probably from watching *Funny Face*—that the Beat era in the 1950s and early 1960s in the Village would have been an amazing time to have a beautiful bookstore.

If you wrote a book, where would you set it in New York, and what famous or notorious New Yorkers would be in the book?
I vowed not to write a book. But I often eat my words and I never say never. My friend Richard Boch, who among his credits was the doorman at the Mudd Club, one day decided to write this book that really touched me. It put in sync all these memories that I had from the Mudd Club days. He did it by recalling stories and also interviewing people who were around then to reconstruct those times. I think that the people I knew, or have known or still know that are a part of my life in New York are the most interesting characters, and I'm big on experience, so it would be all about the people I've met and people I know, and the life and times I've gone through in New York.

When you first started to read books, what was the best place to do so in New York?
I was romantically attached to the idea of sitting on a park bench in Central Park when I lived uptown on the West Side. I thought that was where one goes for peace and quiet and to read a book. But I don't know whether I really enjoyed it or not.

I really enjoy reading books away from noise and in a quiet room. I like the idea of sitting up in a chair, or out in the sun or up on a roof. Anywhere that is quiet and removed from life. I never really read in libraries. I do research there, though. I also love reading in bed before going to sleep.

White Horse Tavern
567 Hudson Street

If you had lived in a cave most of your life and walked into the White Horse Tavern without knowing anything about it whatsoever, you wouldn't necessarily know it is the second oldest continuously operating tavern in all of New York. Even though the bar has preserved much of its original tin ceiling and woodwork, it doesn't feel all that old. It is a pleasant West Village local tavern, and similar to others you may find on Hudson Street. However, you probably do not live in a cave, and I am sure you do know that "The Horse" carries with it an impressive amount of history.

First opened in 1880, this charming West Village locale originally served men working the piers along the Hudson River and was known as a "longshoreman's bar." In the early 1950s, The Horse became a real reunion place for artists and writers. Along with the Lion's Head (an old, defunct Greenwich Village local, which was also an authors' haven), it was a literary hotspot for drinking and mingling among authors.

Dylan Thomas would get very drunk at the White Horse Tavern, and was known to have spent his last few nights there before his death. He was on a poetry-reading tour, and staying at the Chelsea Hotel. A lot of well-known authors from the Beat Generation, most notably Jack Kerouac—who even had his own inscription in the toilet, "JACK GO HOME!"—spent much time drinking here, too. Legend also says the place may or may not be haunted . . . so go and explore to find out for yourself, and we shall see if you report back.

Idlewild
170 Seventh Avenue South

After a recent move from the Flatiron to a much nicer West Village street corner—the ground floor of an amusing-looking building at the southwest intersection of Perry Street and Seventh Avenue—Idlewild is one of the last travel bookstores in the country. Though the shop is focused on travel as a theme and the books are organized by nation, Idlewild also stocks novels and travelogues in an airy and pleasant atmosphere. The staff at Idlewild is more than friendly, and what's more, they also give French, Spanish, Italian, and German lessons in a space attached to the shop.

Fun fact: "Idlewild" was the original name of the New York International Airport, renamed JFK in 1963.

Hotel Albert
23 East 10th Street

I was always a little bit curious about this strange and beautiful building just off of University, my favorite street in all of New York. It seemed slightly odd for some reason, perhaps even haunted, and had a certain mystique around it. Built in 1882 (on top of some 1850 row houses) by Henry Janeway Hardenbergh, the architect of the Dakota and the Plaza, it was converted from apartments to the St. Stephen hotel, which finally became the Hotel Albert in the 1890s. The Albert is famous for attracting many artists and authors: Robert Louis Stevenson was a regular when the Albert was still the St. Stephen; Thomas Wolfe also lived here while teaching at NYU in 1924, and it is said that in *Of Time and the River*, he modeled the Hotel Leopold on the Albert. It was known as a haven in Greenwich Village for artists, and the list of writers who spent time here is endless: Anaïs Nin, Robert Lowell, Horton Foote, Diane di Prima, and Hart Crane, among others. People stayed here for its location and its atmosphere. They would work out of the hotel, and always meet people inside.

Today, The Albert is an apartment building. The five hundred rather seedy hotel rooms were converted into a co-op in 1984. I went to see an apartment that was available once; and if I have some random advice to give anybody, it would be to never try to elucidate a mystery.

Graydon Carter

Cofounder of *Spy*,
former editor-in-chief of *Vanity Fair*,
editor, writer, illustrator, and
Canadian New Yorker

Fray don Carter

Tell me a bit about your personal book collection.
Well, I have most of my books in Connecticut. We have bookshelves in almost every room, it seems. I've read probably 75 percent of the books I have. I reread some of the books. I could probably get rid of 25 percent of the books and not miss them.

I have a lot of the between-the-wars mysteries. I've read hundreds and hundreds of those. I've got every Wodehouse book. I guess I have all the major classics. I have a lot of nonfiction, from the last half century. I have every book ever written on magazines, magazine editors, writers.

Do you think of yourself first and foremost as an illustrator, writer, or editor?
I'm sort of a half-ass at all three. In order of preference of what I like doing: I like drawing, then editing, then writing. Drawing is easy, editing is rather difficult, writing is seriously difficult.

Tell me about Spy.
I started *Spy* eight years after I came to New York, with a friend I made at *Time* magazine, Kurt Andersen. We were both at *Time* and I had an idea for a monthly satirical magazine set in New York about New York. So we combined the writing styles of *Private Eye* and 1940s- and 1950s-era *Time* magazine, which was very adjective-heavy and dense writing, but tried to make it funny at the same time.

It would explain New York. We knew enough about New York to do it—I know ten times more about New York now than I did then. New York was much more of a circus then. The moneyed people showed their money more. They went out to the same restaurants for dinner.

Today, the money is much more vast, but it is hidden in a certain way. It is not as on display, but in those days the characters were big and interesting, much more so than they are now. It had to be a perfect time. New York had been on its uppers for a decade, and roaring back to life, and it roared back to live in a way we didn't fully expect. It was accidental, more than anything.

What is your favorite place to read or write in New York?

To read I actually prefer an upright chair. We have a banquette in our kitchen and I like reading sitting straight up at the kitchen table. That aside, I like lying down on the sofa in our living room and reading. I love to write at the office I have at home. I've never really had an office at home until this one. It's everything I ever dreamt of in a home office.

Home offices can be awfully depressing—those chairs you kneel on with no backs, or bean-bag chairs that strengthen your core. But mine is a wonderful office. I designed it myself. I had it built. It is very modern. It's got everything I love in it. A lot of architectural models and things like that.

Tell me about your most interesting encounter with a New York writer in your career.

Holy shit. There are almost too many. They're all awkward. I have a good one though. For a decade or fifteen years, I used to eat at the same restaurant, Da Silvano —my family had the same table every night. I would bring my kids down. There was a guy across the way, also on a round table on the other side of the door, at table ten. He was often by himself, or with one other friend, sitting at this six-person table. He was lean and had a big head of blond hair, in a sort of 1950s haircut.

A couple of years later, I hired this legendary rock writer named Nick Tosches, who did a wonderful book on Dean Martin, to write a profile on a man named Sydney Korshak, who was the Chicago mob's lawyer in Hollywood. It was one of the most beautiful articles I had ever read. I loved it so much that I called him up and offered to pay him double what I had originally offered. I asked where to send the check, and he said, "Oh, just send it to Da Silvano, that's where I get my mail."

So I asked him if he was the guy across from me for all those years, and he said yes. I asked why he never said hello, and he replied that he didn't want to bother me. After that, we became friends. But while he was writing that article for me, he must have sat across from me about seventy-five times without saying anything, while I was just always intrigued by the mysterious man sitting at the table across from me.

Who for you is the quintessential New York writer?

It's funny, the most quintessential New York writer I know is an illustrator. It's Ed Sorel, who also happens to write beautifully.

CHELSEA, FLATIRON, NOMAD, GRAMERCY & UNION SQUARE

Architecture—the blend of historic townhouses, grand postwar buildings, and sprawling lofts that defines much of historic Manhattan—may be the only common thread uniting the blocks that occupy the late teens and early twenties streets between Downtown and Midtown. Manhattan is supposedly widest across 23rd Street: from west to east, you move from Chelsea to the Flatiron, then on to Gramercy, and finally to the upper region of the residential compound known as Stuyvesant Town–Peter Cooper Village, which borders the East River above the East Village.

As with any place of such breadth and variety, some parts of this region are more delightful to spend time in than others, whose role as an artery of New York City might be geared more toward the practical than the pleasurable. For example, a walk around Gramercy Park to spy through the windows of the National Arts Club or the Players Club, or up Irving Place and the Block Beautiful on 19th Street, can be thrilling, whereas walking up and down Park Avenue, which is only one block away, might be more testing for a pedestrian. Nevertheless, even in those less idyllic parts, you might just stumble upon some hidden literary gems—like one of my absolute favorites, Books of Wonder, which sits right in the middle of "the box region," as I like to call the cluster of chain shops such as the Container Store and Bed, Bath & Beyond, which are packed together around Sixth Avenue. Then there is the hidden General Theological Seminary all the way west, whose garden provides a sanctuary for a lonesome wanderer in search of a good book or somewhere to sit and read.

This slice of Manhattan was also home to many authors. Oscar Wilde lived at 47 Irving Place, on the corner of 17th Street, for a short time; Jack Kerouac wrote *On the Road* at the Chelsea Hotel, and some years later Arthur C. Clarke wrote *2001: A Space Odyssey* there, too. Edith Wharton, the first woman to receive a Pulitzer Prize for Fiction, grew up in a four-story townhouse at 14 West 23rd Street, which I imagine looks very different to what it was at the end of the nineteenth century. The streetscape from Chelsea to Gramercy may have changed since those authors put pen to paper, but, with a great number of New York's best bookstores and literary haunts lining its streets, the area is still a vital one for the bookloving New Yorker.

Posman Books
Chelsea Market: 75 Ninth Avenue
Rockefeller Center: 30 Rockefeller Plaza

Posman Books is one of the country's smallest bookshop chains; two of them are in New York, the other two in Atlanta. Despite its status as a chain, I would most definitely consider Posman an independent bookshop—nothing like a big-name chain, it is family-owned, and the ambiance and selection at their stores are very much those of an independent bookshop. The Posman Books locations in New York perfectly reflect its spirit: unusual, quirky, but still practical.

As an ex-Chelsea resident, I would regularly stop at the Chelsea Market location and get lost in the shop for ages—it's full of great fiction, best sellers, biographies, children's books, as well as cute cards, cool stationery, toys, and great gifts. Posman's other Manhattan location, in Midtown, is equally appealing—and is also in a spirited location, right in the hustle and bustle of Rockefeller Center.

Goethe-Institut
30 Irving Place

Irving Place—which is reminiscent of a quaint London high street—was named after Washington Irving, the nineteenth-century American short-story writer and essayist. He was greatly admired in Europe and by the likes of Lord Byron, Charles Dickens, and Walter Scott. Credited as the first American Man of Letters, Irving—who was himself named after George Washington—had Irving Place named after him while he was still alive.

If you walk up Irving Place just a couple of blocks north of 14th Street, you will discover the Goethe-Institut. For any Germanophile New Yorker, this place is most likely in their regular rotation. But for anybody who has never really come across it, this is an ideal place to take up German lessons, research the culture, or soak all of it up in their lovely library.

As in most libraries, if you wish to borrow some of their German books and bring them home, you will need a membership. If you simply wish to browse, though, the place is here for the taking and open to the public. In a great neighborhood full of literary wealth, take a minute to enjoy the best of Germany in New York—learn the language, get a sense of contemporary German fiction, or attend classes and events celebrating German literary culture. Please note: the library is closed during the summertime, from the end of June until early September.

Barnes & Noble
33 East 17th Street
555 5th Avenue
2289 Broadway

There was a time when Barnes & Noble was labeled Public Enemy #1 by New York's small bookshop owners. Today, for many, that honor goes to Amazon and other online platforms, while Barnes & Noble ironically has found itself in its own precarious position, clinging on as a brick-and-mortar bastion for booklovers.

It all began in 1873, from Charles M. Barnes's home in Wheaton, Illinois, where the eponymous book business was first set up. Barnes's son William joined forces with G. Clifford Noble in New York, in 1917, and thus was born the great Barnes & Noble. Its flagship shop was originally located in the Flatiron, on Fifth Avenue and 18th Street. In the mid-1970s, Barnes & Noble proved itself to be an innovator and became the first bookseller in America to offer discounted books. That was a significant part of its huge expansion to the northeastern markets, shortly followed by the additions of Bookmasters, Marboro Books, B. Dalton Bookseller, Doubleday Book Shops, and BookStop to their empire. In the late 1980s, Barnes & Noble was the second largest bookstore in America. It was not until the 1990s, though, that Barnes & Noble established its modern generation of superstores as we now know them.

Today, the chain's most notable store in Manhattan sits in a grand building that presides over the hustle and bustle of Union Square. Another branch of the superstore, on Fifth Avenue between 45th and 46th Streets in Midtown, is almost as prominent—but the size, selection, and grandeur of the Union Square branch makes it unquestionably the company's flagship. Inside, readers and shoppers will find floor upon floor of stacks broken out into various themes and categories, from an entire floor of fiction to walls of art books and entire hallways of biographies. The store has adapted to the twenty-first-century vision of a bookstore, with peripheral big-bookshop departments supplementing the vast selection of books—large toy sections where kids can meet or play or gather around for special story times (like the famed Christmas pajama one), really nice stationery and calendar sections to find gifts or treats for yourself, and sections filled with DVDs, CDs, and magazines.

The Union Square shop has a sweet spot in my heart—not just because I have a crush on Union Square as a location in itself, but also because its building feels so majestic. I should also confess that one of my favorite items on display at Barnes & Noble is a pile of surprise books: a book is wrapped up in a beautiful little package and you can pick one by genre to give as a present without ever knowing what it is! Last time I was there, I had a long chat with the young woman who personally chooses the books and then wraps them individually and caringly—proving that yes, there is still heart and soul even in those big superstore chains you might have other preconceived ideas about.

Pete's Tavern
129 East 18th Street

On the corner of 18th Street and the ever so pleasant and noiseless Irving Place is an establishment you will want to visit and enjoy: Pete's Tavern, also known as "The Tavern O. Henry made famous"—a fact you won't be able to miss, as it is clearly inscribed along its black awning.

O. Henry, who had deep affection for New York and called it "Baghdad-on-the-Subway," was not the only author who wrote and drank at Pete's Tavern. Funnily enough, my utter favorite artist of all time, Ludwig Bemelmans, wrote the first lines of *Madeline* at Pete's. Though inscribed on a "Friends of Libraries U.S.A." plaque just outside the bar's door, Pete's Tavern had been my local long before I even discovered this. Perhaps that is what subconsciously drew me to this place—oh, and maybe the fact that it is actually a true local: the atmosphere is chock-full of spirit, the drinks and food are not bad either, and the staff there is wonderful because the place has been family-owned for so long.

I sat down with Gary Egan, who has been Pete's delightfully friendly manager for the past thirty years, and asked him what we all need to know.

What sets Pete's Tavern apart from the other historical bars in New York?
Well, we are the longest continuously operating bar and restaurant in New York City. We've been open since 1864, and have never closed since then. We were open throughout Prohibition, and that was due to the proximity of Tammany Hall, which was located on 17th Street, between Irving and Park. We were disguised as a florist throughout Prohibition.

Are there any secrets nobody knows about Pete's Tavern?
We have the old dummy refrigerator door hinges still here, and the old side doors are still visible—it says "127" on top, which was the address. The whole place is quite historical as it is, but there are no real big secrets.

Who is the man with glasses in all the photos on the wall with celebrities?
He's the general manager, same as myself, and we have both been here for thirty years. The place is family owned and always has been.

What's the best part about working at such an institution as Pete's?
The staff is like a family, it's run like a family. Everybody has been here a long time, and the clientele is great. You get a real mixture of people, from twenty-two years of age to ninety sitting at the bar. You get locals, you get tourists, you get business people. It's a nice mix of people.

I sometimes wish the building was a little less old, just for upkeep. It's more difficult to keep an old place old than a new place new. You don't necessarily want to change things, and sometimes that can be difficult. We got a leak in the ceiling from above once, and it took a month to find the same tiles. We take a lot of pride in maintaining the historical aspect of the place, and sometimes it's difficult to do that. The old globes in the chandelier up there also took us a month to find. Old New York is tricky to keep up.

What makes this place such a literary landmark?

The first lines of *Madeline* were written here, as was *The Gift of the Magi*. The ambiance and the neighborhood really help. Everything around Gramercy Park also contributes to that—the Players Club, the National Arts Club . . . Don't forget, in the late 1800s to early 1900s, this used to be considered "uptown." The great thing about this Gramercy Park area is that it has survived, and that is thanks to the Landmarks Preservation Commission. We were designated a landmark in 1966, and so there's no neon signs, none of that. You step one block over to Park Avenue and it is commonplace New York, same on the other side of Third Avenue, whereas this is such a little special pocket of New York.

Any literary anecdotes about this place?

The great thing, really, is we have all the memorabilia in the O. Henry booth—we have the letter he wrote to his brother, and another letter he wrote declining an invitation to dinner. They really are cherished pieces, which are handwritten by him.

The O. Henry booth is booked solid for the next year. You get people from all corners of the world, it is a fantastic thing. You know, I studied O. Henry in Ireland when I grew up, and we read the short story "The Green Door" in school. To actually think that I was a schoolboy in Ireland at the age of fourteen and studied this man that would later become almost like my legacy is truly fantastic. I know he is on the English syllabus in Japan, in China, in Australia . . . that is such a legacy in itself.

Same goes for Ludwig Bemelmans. Isn't it great to look back after all these years and find a place where these authors went so often? I give it to the Landmarks Preservation Commission. It's great that people get to come in here, eat, drink, soak up the atmosphere—it's unique, it's different than just visiting a place in a museum or a library.

Books of Wonder
18 West 18th Street

Books of Wonder seems like it has the ability to pull in anybody from the real world (i.e. 18th Street) and transport them to any world of their choosing via their vast selection of children's treasures. Without trying to seem extravagant, I would suggest that if you were to set out to create an urban literary Disneyland fabricated only of books, Books of Wonder would be it. I mean that in the best possible way—this bookshop is simply a magical and transcendent place, both for children and for the adults who bring them here.

After having moved locations a few times since 1980, Books of Wonder's current space is big enough to serve as a special home to every single imaginable children's book you have ever wanted, needed, or happened upon. Very centrally located in the middle of the Flatiron District, the rather airy ground-floor shop is currently in the biggest location the store has inhabited yet, and it also has a little café area to the right of the shop and an exhibit section in the back with art and rare editions, all of which I believe are for sale (I found a Sendak *Where the Wild Things Are* listed on their website for $22,500). The shop is also very well equipped with book-related gifts, such as tote bags, baby clothes, those cool tees with book covers on them, and soft toys. They regularly host events, which draw crowds that completely fill up the huge shop—which isn't surprising when you consider they manage to get authors such as J. K. Rowling (twice!) through the door for signings and talks.

As if I didn't already love it enough, I recently discovered that Books of Wonder was the real-life bookshop Nora Ephron based the *You've Got Mail* store on (definitely in the top five of my favorite films). Meg Ryan "practiced" in the shop before they started shooting, and staff from Books of Wonder went to the film set to help make sure it looked authentic. As a rom-com super-fan, this was extremely exciting for me. Whether you have a kid or not, Books of Wonder is one of the best bookshops around—and aren't we all still kids inside, anyway?

John at 7th Avenue & 19th Street
Southeast corner of 19th Street and 7th Avenue, Chelsea

Every evening, I walk across town (approximately from Tenth Avenue to Third Avenue). Sometimes I take 21st Street, other times 20th, and on some rare occasions I walk down 19th Street, which is probably my favorite. 19th Street is home to the FDNY Engine 3/Tower Ladder 12/Battalion 7, and my son and I like stopping by to see if they are open or not; when they are, we chat and enjoy how welcoming the firefighters are. 19th Street is also home to a book vendor, who sits on the corner, and whom I also like chatting with, whether it is about books, the area, life in general, or the weather.

John is an old man, somewhere between fifty-nine and ninety-two—it's completely impossible to tell. He has a long white beard, long hair, and a permanent grin. He is very friendly and rather cute, in a distant-grandfather or Father-Christmas kind of way. I often stop and look at his book collection. I look at him. I wonder what his life story is. I wonder where he came from. I wonder where he got his books. Sometimes I wonder what John will do after he packs up. I'll never know. I don't ask. Once I bought a Japanese home décor book from John. It was three dollars. He offered me a notebook to go with it, which he claimed was "part of the same set"—the two for a total of five dollars. I said yes. I like those two things; I have them at home.

Andrew Heiskell Braille & Talking Book Library
40 West 20th Street

The Andrew Heiskell Braille and Talking Book Library is not only one of the best-equipped providers of services for the blind and the visually impaired in the country—it's also one of the most pleasant lending libraries in the city. As well as stocking books and magazines in braille, the library carries a large selection of talking books and even houses an audio studio where volunteers can record audio-books, and is equipped with magnifying readers and adaptive computer technology to bring literature of all kinds to visually impaired readers of every level.

As a person who is not visually impaired, I have used the Heiskell on a few occasions the way I would any other library, and it has been nothing but agreeable and efficient. The staff was awfully friendly (much more so than in certain other libraries), and so were the people using the facilities there. I know someone (not visually impaired either) who was merely walking out of the library after returning a DVD, and was gently escorted out of the building by a fellow library goer just for wearing sunglasses. Not knowing quite what to do, and slightly taken aback by the situation, he told me he just went with it in order not to upset the kind person who'd been so helpful.

Centrally located in the Flatiron, the library also has quite a cute baby room in an almost separate section right in the front, so I would definitely recommend it if you have a little one who needs enter-taining while you explore the shelves. The spacious room and sofas in the back are also great if you need somewhere to study or to take a minute to read (or listen) in peace.

The National Arts Club
15 Gramercy Park South

Founded in 1898 by Charles De Kay, who was not just an author and poet, but also the literary and art critic for the *New York Times*, the National Arts Club was a place of gathering for artists, art lovers, and patrons of the arts of all genres. The Club took residence in a mansion on 34th Street before outgrowing it in 1906, and moving to its current Gramercy Park location. Formerly known as the home of Governor Samuel J. Tilden—whose extensive personal book collection helped build the foundation for the New York Public Library—the mansion that is now home to The National Arts Club was designed by Calvert Vaux (who is not only the name behind Central Park, but also the Jefferson Market Courthouse, which is now a library) and perfectly reflects the spirit of the Club. In addition to three U.S. Presidents— Theodore Roosevelt, Woodrow Wilson, and Dwight D. Eisenhower— the Club's membership has included countless artists, ranging from well-known painters to authors alike.

Today, the National Arts Club hosts members-only events, as well as events open to the general public. Some of those include exhibitions, theatrical and musical performances, lectures, and readings, all of which focus on various disciplines of the arts. Countless literary parties and book launches have been hosted at the Club.

The National Arts Club also awards Medals of Honor to leading figures in their respective chosen fields of art. Since 1968, the Medal of Honor for Literature's mission has been "to present literary works of merit to the membership and to the general public through readings and discussions with authors, panel discussions on literary subjects of interest, and by introducing promising new authors." Some of the literary honorees over the years have included such prestigious authors as Tennessee Williams, Norman Mailer, Saul Bellow, Allen Ginsberg, Isaac Bashevis Singer, John Updike, Marguerite Yourcenar, Philip Roth, Margaret Atwood, Tom Wolfe, Edna O'Brien, Alice Munro, Don DeLillo, Joyce Carol Oates, Martin Amis, Salman Rushdie, and Paul Auster, among many others.

When I first had the honor and privilege of sitting in the clubhouse's beautiful Parlor (and legally this time, as I must confess that I have tried to get drinks there unsuccessfully on a few occasions in the past), I met with the delightful and very elegant president of the Club, Linda Zagaria; the Club's registrar and principal archivist, Robert Yahner; and the general manager, John Eramo.

Tell me about the literary program you have here.

There is a very active literary committee here. We award a Medal of Honor in each art category, and the one for literature is probably the most well known. Just this year, the award was given to John McPhee, the nonfiction author who also writes for the *New Yorker*. It was a stellar evening. David Remnick was there, as was Mary Norris. Literary luminaries came out in force to honor John McPhee, who was, fittingly, wearing a fishing vest to his own black-tie event. The previous winner in 2017 was Alexander McCall Smith, who came dressed all in tartan. Of course, the event was major news back in Edinburgh.

We host one or two literary events at the National Arts Club per month, whether it is a book presentation or a launch. For example, in May 2018 we hosted a conversation with André Aciman; a literary member conducted the interview, and the event was sold out. In the mid-1990s, the Club was really popular for book launches. A lot of authors had book parties here. It was a very popular thing to do: the National Arts Club would host and the authors would provide the books. A lot of people would come; you would get to meet the author in an intimate setting. A lot of great authors have walked through the Club. We have autographed copies of all the books from those parties in our archives. There are a great number of them. There is also a great amount of correspondence between the Club and Tennessee Williams, Eudora Welty, Marguerite Yourcenar. They are not openly available to the public, but people can make an appointment to come and see them. Once a year, though, we do put on an archive show, which people can come and see. Everybody is usually totally fascinated.

Are there any secrets in the archives?

Nothing earth-shattering. It is wonderful to see how open this place is, with such magnificent art, yet nothing has been stolen since the 1960s. There was the Paul Manship that was stolen and returned a decade later. The archives do, however, hold a lot of interesting stuff and gossipy stories, which everybody loves.

How is the Poetry Society of America connected to the club?

The Poetry Society of America was founded here in 1910. At the time, there was space available for them to move in and grow with the Club. Today, they still have an office here, but it is smaller. Poets that are members of the Society can just drop in.

Tell me about the rooms at the Club, and how many pieces of literary work you think have been written here?

There are fourteen rooms available for rent in the Club, six of which are "old style." When Tilden was the Governor, he had rooms here, and a lot of guests would stay overnight. The parlor in the Clubhouse was the first room that made up Tilden's library, and the blue glaze that is still here was part of Tilden's library.

Ludwig Bemelmans certainly wrote a lot here. He lived in an apartment on the twelfth floor, in which he painted some murals. Following his residency, the woman who took over and lived there for three decades was Tony Zwicker, an important dealer in artists' books. She sold works by Matisse, Joseph Beuys, etc., and worked from up there with Barry Scott, also a dealer in antiquarian and rare books—one of the most important dealers of

European and American first editions. Many important literary people visited the twelfth-floor studio. Dianne Bernhard, a former Club president and Fine Arts Committee member, lives there now, and the Bemelmans murals are still up there. Lillian Hoban—the creator of the *Frances* children's books series—also lived there. Unlike Eloise in the Plaza, Frances did not live at the National Arts Club, but in the suburbs of Connecticut.

What is one of the best literary anecdotes associated with the Club?

Well, the essence of the original New York Public Library, Astor, Lenox, and Tilden Foundations were made of the books which lived in these rooms. In a way, a part of what is now known as the NYPL began here. In fact, the NYPL holds many of Tilden's papers in its archives.

We have remnants here of the original National Arts Club library. Parts of Tilden's collection, which he did not donate to the New York Public Library, have stayed in his original bookcases, and we have them upstairs in a private office for research purposes and for archivists.

Who are some of the most famous literary characters who have set foot in the Club?

There have been so many . . . But I guess Allen Ginsberg, Saul Bellow, and John Updike.

What is the most attractive piece of history associated with the Club?

The list of early members and founders is quite exciting. To be a member of a club that those people also were members of is quite something.

The Clubhouse itself, the actual structure, is part of one of the most unique aesthetic movements, and has its own style within the Gothic aesthetic. Tilden hired Calvert Vaux, who ornamented the house with leaves, birds, and flowers, so that in itself is very magical.

I like to imagine life when Tilden was still governor. He was very sociable. Also, I believe the Club was still open during Prohibition, and there were tunnels in the basement that led to 19th Street and the Players Club, and I think there was a lot of back and forth, and I like to imagine what went on back then.

Where is the best place to read in the Club, or in the neighborhood?

The window seat in this parlor, looking at Gramercy Park, is inspirational, especially in the winter during a snowy afternoon. Also, Stuyvesant Park is a local hidden treasure where it is nice to read. It used to be Peter Stuyvesant's farm.

What would be the most appropriate book to read at the Club?

Anything by Edith Wharton would fit the Club's atmosphere very well. *Time and Again* would also be great.

The Christoph Keller, Jr. Library at the General Theological Seminary

440 West 21st Street

Hidden all the way in the depths of West Chelsea are some of the most magnificent blocks you will ever come across in New York. In a long and wide plot surrounded with grand townhouses and old-fashioned apartment buildings, between Ninth and Tenth Avenues and 20th and 21st Streets, is the General Theological Seminary. Nestled behind the imposing grandeur of the Highline Hotel's Collegiate Gothic construction (formerly the Seminary Campus) and protected by somewhat unnoticeable but intriguing iron fences and gates are the grounds of this mysterious and beautiful Seminary.

It was Clement Clarke Moore, the author of *A Visit from St. Nicholas*, who donated sixty-six tracts of land—the apple orchard from his inherited Chelsea estate—to become the site of the new Seminary, which moved there in 1827. Around the corner from the Seminary, Clement Clarke Moore now has a park named after him—also known as Seal Park to the local children, for the seal fountains that spray the playground in the summer.

Dare to enter the Seminary—you will need to show your ID at the entrance to do so, and provide a valid reason for your visit—and you will be mesmerized by its beauty and the abundance of green that the Seminary's Close has to offer within the premises. Walk past its beautiful Episcopal church and the rest of its impressive neo-Gothic buildings toward Ninth Avenue, and you will encounter the more modern 1960s Chelsea Enclave, which recently replaced Sherrill Hall (due to some financial problems the Seminary was facing). Enter that construction, bear an immediate right, and there you will find the Keller Library, which, although not a lending library, is open to the public to stroll in and have a quiet wander or read in. Visiting scholars, clergy, and laypeople may use the library's resources for research and reference.

The Christoph Keller, Jr. Library at the General Seminary is the oldest Episcopal seminary library, and a "magnificent treasury of books, manuscripts, records, and source materials for the study of the life and thought of Christianity," according to Niels Henry Sonne. "To form the proud commencement of a Library," John Pintard, an early New York civic leader, raised $330 to donate "the only set of the Fathers now for sale in America" to the General Theological Seminary in 1820. Since then, the library has boasted an important collection of ancient and English Bibles, which includes a Hebrew Bible dating all the way to 1264, a Latin one from 1250, and three tenth-century Gospels. The library once had a Gutenberg Bible, which it acquired in 1898; one of the pages appeared to have been forged, so it was replaced with a page from another incomplete copy, making it the first incomplete Gutenberg Bible to be made whole again. It reportedly sold for $2.2 million to the Württembergische Landesbibliothek in Stuttgart in 1978.

Library

192 Books
192 Tenth Avenue

I always loved 192 Books for its true local bookshop feel. It is almost out of a film. Perfectly sized, cute, and "neighborhoody," it was really something nice to have one block away from where we lived when I first became a mother and had to deal with the daily loneliness, boredom, and fatigue. The displays here are immaculate, the service is wonderful, and the quality of the selection is not at all bad, either, encompassing everything from a well-curated list of contemporary and classic fiction to new art monographs, a substantial shelf of poetry, and even a great collection of children's books.

Having relocated directly east, I don't spend as much time here now as I used to—but one little person who does is my son. His daycare is around the corner. Although he is only three and doesn't communicate very clearly what they do at school, every evening the loving teachers send back a note with the children's daily activities—and Wednesdays are my favorite. The mini boys and girls leave the daycare grounds holding hands two-by-two and go for story time at 192. Lisa, the storyteller, is apparently a truly wonderful person. She reads incredibly captivating tales to all the children and they listen voraciously and then pester her with questions. "But why? But why?"

When I ask my son about Lisa, his face lights up. I feel like half of it is him thinking of her fondly and loving her, and the other half might be him wondering how I know about her, and how on earth I managed to infiltrate the secret little world he thought he had kept me out of. I was torn about what to do. One part of me wanted to meet Lisa; but another part of me just wanted to know her through my son and his teachers—as the wondrous, most patient, generous, beautifully spoken, fairytale-reading creature from 192 Books.

Gramercy Typewriter Company
108 West 17th Street

Abraham Schweitzer first opened the Gramercy Typewriter Company in 1932 in the little basement of a townhouse in Gramercy Park. Now in its third generation of owners (all from the same Schweitzer family, of course), the Gramercy Typewriter Company is known for providing New York with excellent typewriter repairs and services, as well as offering expert advice on some of the very best typewriters, which they also have for sale.

After forty-seven years in the Flatiron building, Paul Schweitzer (Abraham's son), Paul's son Jay, and their friendly staff are now only a short walk away on 17th Street. The little shop is full of absolutely gorgeous machines—a couple of pale pink and blue Royals, a red Valentine (the same one they have in the permanent collection at the MoMA), and all kinds of Olympias and Olivettis, all of which you can buy. There are also lots of other machines, dropped off and waiting to be repaired, that you can have a look at—on a recent visit, one of them happened to be Tom Hanks's.

You can ask Schweitzer all about the shop and the company's history while you listen to him type away invoices, repair slips, or whatever else he has to write up on his own machine. It's a splendid and novel place to stop by when the writer in you is inspired by all the bookshops you've visited and demands a machine with which to finally hammer out that novel . . . Or perhaps your current machine needs some work done to it, and you can go in for a reassuring chat about all the other authors who have been in with their own typewriters in need of an update.

Hotel Chelsea
222 West 23rd Street

It is difficult to know where to begin with the Hotel Chelsea—also sometimes called the Chelsea, or the Chelsea Hotel, which I prefer to use. The physical building is still here, but most of its soul and character seem to be gone. Its rich history and distinct charm still have a certain presence and an aura that floats above 23rd Street, but it would be impossible ever to try and recapture what the Chelsea Hotel embodied in its heyday. The list of authors that lived or spent time here is endless, and the stories we have all heard or read are as fantastic and unbelievable as one could ever possibly imagine.

Here is just a quick snapshot of the many literary legends for whom the Chelsea provided a home: O. Henry, Jack Kerouac, Dylan Thomas (who spent some of his last nights here after drinking at the White Horse Tavern and before being hospitalized and passing away), Jean-Paul Sartre, Simone de Beauvoir (a hero to most people, but especially to any writing French woman, of course), Charles Bukowski, Allen Ginsberg, William S. Burroughs, and Mark Twain, among many others. Arthur C. Clarke is known to have written *2001: A Space Odyssey* at the Chelsea.

Today, the status of the Chelsea Hotel is in permanent turmoil. There has been scaffolding over it for as long as I can remember, and stories as to its future are often conflicted. A friend of my sister's stayed there on a visit to New York nearly a decade ago. We took him with us to a wedding in Woodstock, and I remember him telling us how excited he was to be at the Chelsea due to its history, its old-school charm, and everything else it had to offer culturally and intellectually—he seemed to be absolutely thrilled about it. But when we drove him back to the city, he went to the reception desk to ask for his key only to find all his belongings packed up: the hotel had enforced an unexplained early checkout for all the guests. The management and ownership had abruptly changed, and not much further information was given to anybody. That anecdote always stuck in my memory, and, to me, perfectly matches the romanticism and mystery of the place.

I was fortunate enough to speak to author Ed Hamilton, who still lives in the Chelsea and has written extensively about it.

Dylan Thomas

You still live in the Chelsea Hotel. When you first moved there in 1995 after seeing an ad in the newspaper, was it as you expected?

It far exceeded my expectations. I loved it immediately because it was my ideal of bohemian heaven. All kinds of people passing through, some staying for a long time and some for the night. There was an unspoken rule that you could just wander into whatever party you wanted to. It was a very accepting place.

What was the best thing about living there? And the worst?

It was a little bit scary because, in addition to the artists and writers, there were all these crazy characters, schizophrenics and junkies and prostitutes.

What's the craziest thing that has ever happened in the Chelsea Hotel during your time as a resident there?

Rocker Dee Dee Ramone was about the craziest person I've met at the Chelsea. He was staying next door to me, and I didn't know it was him. There were construction workers upstairs, and he started banging on my wall, "Shut up, shut up!" Then he came to my door, dressed in just his jockey shorts and covered in tattoos. He said, "Shut up with that racket!" I said, "It's not me, Dee Dee. It's those guys upstairs." He ran back into his room and threw open his window and started yelling at them, "You shut up, up there! Motherfuckers! I'll come up there and kill you!" Of course they deliberately made more noise, and that just drove him nuts.

What is the best place to read or write in Chelsea? Where is the best place to get books?

192 Books is a great indie bookstore located in Chelsea. I go to bookstores all over the city. I buy a lot of books; I would have more, but it's such a small apartment. Sometimes I have to set them out, unfortunately.

Aside from your book, what are some good reads about the Chelsea Hotel, or the neighborhood, or even New York?

Sherrill Tippins's *Inside the Dream Palace: The Life and Times of New York's Legendary Chelsea Hotel* is a must for fans of the hotel. For a book about what's happening in contemporary New York, check out Jeremiah Moss's *Vanishing New York: How a Great City Lost Its Soul.*

Where will you live after the Chelsea Hotel?

It's hard to say where I'd end up if I had to leave the Chelsea. This place is synonymous with my experience in New York. This is the last outpost of bohemianism in New York. I intend to stay as long as I can.

Swann Auction Galleries
104 East 25th Street

Following its first auction on March 27, 1942, and dedicated to rare and antiquarian books, Swann has since become the largest auction house in the world of works on paper. It is New York's oldest specialty auction house and sells anything whatsoever on paper, with the exceptions of currency and stamps. Swann Galleries is now a third-generation family business. If you are a true booklover and collector, you might consider looking into visiting Swann Galleries or attending one of their (approximately) forty sales a year.

After seventy-seven years in business, Swann is a place made "of collectors, for collectors," as its current president and principal auctioneer Nicholas Lowry mentions; at Swann, they deal with "material we love, selling it to people who love it as much as we do."

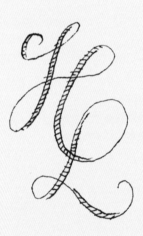

Rizzoli Bookstore
1133 Broadway

First opened in 1964 at 712 Fifth Avenue, the original Rizzoli Bookstore rubbed shoulders with the likes of the Plaza, Tiffany's, and Bergdorf Goodman. It was designed by the architect Ferdinand Gottlieb, and its iconic interior featured in quite the list of Hollywood films, one of which was Woody Allen's *Manhattan*. Angelo Rizzoli, the founder, was in fact also a film producer (working on *La Dolce Vita* with Federico Fellini, among others), as well as a publisher. In 1974, Rizzoli New York launched its publishing operation as we know it today, and its reputation in the art, fashion, culinary, design, and photography worlds is second to none.

After nearly thirty years in its second location—the famed and beloved 57th Street townhouse, which was sadly demolished amid protests and complaints from everybody—Rizzoli moved slightly downtown to welcome bibliophiles, art lovers, tourists, locals, readers, and wanderers of all ages in its new yet homey, sophisticated, and spacious location in the St. James Building. Nestled in a trendy and bustling part of the Flatiron—also known as NoMad (North of Madison Square Park)—the latest incarnation of the Rizzoli Bookstore (open since 2015) is everything you would expect, and more. Its new neighbors are the delicious Eataly, the colorful Marimekko and, of course, everybody's favorite LEGO store.

Despite how majestic and special Rizzoli might feel, with its high ceilings, its wooden shelves, its marble floors, its intricate Fornasetti murals, and its thoughtfully laid-out book displays, there is also a very cozy and intimate feeling to the store. All the way in the back, there is a wonderful room—reminiscent of the big ballroom my grandparents never had, where I would have fantasized of secretly playing hide and seek, or of a games room with a beautiful billiards table and comfy armchairs to fall asleep in—which accommodates more ponderous shoppers by day and signings, launches, and other events by night. Yet again, despite all of its grandness and majesty, that room, along with the rest of the bookshop, has something intrinsically warm and comforting about it—perhaps because of the amalgamation of all the inviting piles and shelves of books on art, architecture, photography, cooking, and fashion that surround you.

The bookshop has something for everybody: your playful kids, your fun artsy friends, your fancy friends, your cool Downtown friends, your intellectual grandparents, or perhaps just yourself. If you're in search of the latest, greatest work of fiction, or a nice New York souvenir you want to carry around in one of Rizzoli's lovely and sturdy signature green totes, a trip to the Rizzoli Bookstore is more than worthwhile, I would say—and I promise I am not biased!

Charles Miers

Publisher of Rizzoli

What does your personal book collection look like, and what are some of your most valuable and prized books?

For me, books are old friends and walks down memory lane. I started collecting illustrated books in high school, especially photography and art monographs, and now have sizable collections of architecture, photography, fashion, art, and interior design books, as well as books on New York, greatly magnified by the many books I have had the good fortune to publish. Of the Rizzoli books, some are publishing milestones, some are limited editions, some are great reference books, some have very creative inscriptions or even drawings by artists—all memorable.

I suppose besides the ones I have published, my most prized books are those of only personal value: family Bibles, books my parents owned that I grew up with, schoolbooks and yearbooks, and old novels, the more thumbed and yellowed the better.

Now if I could only take one book to a desert island, it would be my *Times Atlas of the World*, which I use all the time, to dream mostly. It's full of possibility and intrigue, and rich with both surprise and familiarity. Its wonderful oversized format and pages demand ambitious thinking and suggest the world is impossible to hold in two arms. Unlike armchair travel, I read it on the floor usually, like you would a map, physically engaged.

How much and what type of books do you read for leisure, or is your personal reading life completely intertwined with your professional one?

I have to be very involved in the subjects we publish, but this is as much through magazines as books. I'm always very, very far behind on my personal reading; something really has to catch my attention from a review . . . usually history or travel with a strong narrative, or history specific to a place I have traveled to, or to New York, which is such a literary city, or related to a film I have seen . . . sometimes a political book or a novel everyone is reading, so I keep up. That said, I frequently am reading or hearing a phrase or line and wanting to know more about its source, so I'm often diving back into literary classics or historical references for a couple of hours.

What changes did you make in the mission of Rizzoli when you took over the reins?

I think Rizzoli has always stood for a certain level of taste and high bookmaking standards and I have done my best to maintain those values.

I have encouraged our authors and art directors to make books that are unique and that are as expressive of their subjects and as exquisite as possible—and I hope I have given them the tools to do so. My tenure has co-incided with a moment when people particularly value and cherish the tactile qualities of the book, and I have tried to pronounce this in the way we publish.

Our range of subjects has greatly expanded, as has our list, from fifty books a year to almost two hundred. And my tastes and interests are much more varied than my predecessors'. Where once we were known to be a world leader in architecture only, now we are world leaders in fashion, in interior design, in art books. We publish a great many celebrities; we also have a very strong New York list; we even have a growing outdoors and environmental list.

What are the most enjoyable parts of your work at Rizzoli?
Without a doubt interacting with and learning from some of the world's most visually creative people. Our subjects, our authors, and our art directors are my heroes, and their exceptional visual sensibility is why we publish their work. Their involvement in and approach to a book is always an education for me. The individual vision, care, and attention they bring are what make Rizzoli successful.

And I love going to bookstores, especially ours! We are very proud to still have a flagship book-store on the same scale we have maintained since the 1970s. Whether being in Avery Library at Columbia or at the Metropolitan Museum or in Urban Outfitters or the Strand, anywhere that has lots of books is like a candy store for me.

What are some characteristics a publishing house needs in order to run seamlessly and produce great literary and artistic works?
Great subjects and authors willing to invest their creativity in book form. Excellent editors who believe in and wish to share their enthusiasms and tastes. Brilliant graphic designers or art directors whose hand, whether very subtle and traditional or overt and flamboyant, helps create a worthy, memorable object. A production team ever willing to push the envelope of what a book should be. A sales force and marketing and publicity teams who believe unconditionally in all of the above. The extraordinary support of booksellers, who often know our books almost as well as we do, and always know our readers much better than we do . . . And owners who for thirty years have trusted me to keep the jewel that is Rizzoli shining brightly.

What does the perfect book look like in your mind?
Its physical form—its format, paper, binding, and typography—expresses its subject matter perfectly.

Did you always want to work in the book world?
I think what sold me was going to my first job interview and seeing the wall of books behind the publisher's desk. To have such a physical and intellectual manifestation of one's work was inspiring. And I've always loved rare books . . . or what we call "vintage books" nowadays.

If you weren't the publisher of Rizzoli, what would you be doing?
Probably trying to be the publisher of Rizzoli.

Printed Matter, Inc.
231 11th Avenue

NY Art Book Fair
Once a year, for a few days in September at MoMA PS1
22-25 Jackson Avenue on 46th Avenue, Long Island City

One of my first real "grown-up" apartments was in Chelsea. I was madly in love with the place and the building, but did not care so much for the area: all the way "up" in the 20s, super far west, with inhabitants a little bit older in age than I was at the time . . . The whole scene was not mine, and it was quite removed from what I used to characterize as Downtown (SoHo, Chinatown, the East and West Villages, etc.). Except as soon as I moved there, I instantly felt at home. I adored it. Everything about it was perfect. It was close to the water, and the West Side had recently been completely redeveloped, so walking from Chelsea all the way down to TriBeCa was one of the most pleasant strolls you could take.

Then there were all these streets in the teens and the low 20s, which were made up of rows of large and beautiful old townhouses. It felt like the West Village or London, except it was better, because the pavements were wider and you were in America. There was also the Highline, the Chelsea Market, lots of nice coffee shops and new restaurants, the Chelsea Hotel, and history everywhere you looked. To top it off, there were loads of galleries with cool exhibitions. After having a baby, everything I just mentioned came in really handy when all I had left of my humanity and my sanity was taking a walk with a pram, which seemed to contain a continuous crying machine.

That's when I discovered Printed Matter, Inc. At the time it was on Tenth Avenue between 21st and 22nd streets; and in fact, with said pram, it was not completely ideal. There were so many stands and shelves and all these artists' books I had yet to discover. The shop was filled with too many cool and young people. I felt a bit old and like a granny—definitely not trendy enough. But it didn't really matter, because Printed Matter is very open and welcoming to everybody. I went there a lot, and I enjoyed it. Nowadays, it has moved up to Eleventh Avenue and 26th Street. Not only that, it has actually expanded and opened a new, cozier branch in the Swiss Institute in the East Village.

Printed Matter was founded as a nonprofit in 1976. It is dedicated to "the dissemination, the understanding, and the appreciation of artists' books and related publications." The organization was first established in TriBeCa by a group of individuals working in the arts (Sol LeWitt was one of them), and it was developed to cater to the growing demand for publications made by artists. Printed Matter moved to SoHo in 1989, and to Chelsea in 2001, which, by then, was already the official New York hub for contemporary art. Today, Printed Matter also happens to be the brains and the machinery behind the prestigious New York Art Book Fair, which occupies the Museum of Modern Art's contemporary outpost, PS1, in Long Island City every September.

It seemed only fitting to ask Max Schumann, Printed Matter's executive director, all that we should know about this legendary institution.

How many books do you think there are on Printed Matter's shelves? What percentage of them have you read versus the percentage you have never touched or opened?

We have approximately twelve thousand titles in stock, and approximately sixty thousand titles have been represented by Printed Matter since its founding in 1976. Because I managed the store's annual inventory count for more than twenty years, I've probably touched and opened a healthy majority of the titles. Reading artists' books can be very different from reading conventional forms of literature; opening and flipping through artists' books is a form of artists'-book reading. We had approximately 380 exhibitors at the last New York Art Book Fair, from more than thirty countries. I'd estimate at least ten thousand titles were represented at the fair.

What prompted you to join Printed Matter?

In the 1980s, I was involved in the cheap art movement, making and selling art at ridiculously low prices. My sister was assistant manager at Printed Matter and got me a job packing books during the holidays. That was in 1989 and I never left—it was the perfect place for me!

What is the most expensive book you carry? What is the rarest book you have ever stocked?

Our mission is to distribute artists' books to the broadest audience possible—and that means that we are mostly selling books that are very affordable. That's the beauty of artists' books—that they are accessible and affordable. Having said that, we also do carry rare books in order to be able to provide the rich historical context (and it also is nice to sell a book for $1,000 every once in a while, which would be equivalent to selling a hundred $10 books!). Ed Ruscha's *Dutch Details* is very rare, most of the edition was destroyed. We've had that once or twice during my near-thirty years at Printed Matter. And recently we had a signed copy of Bruce Nauman's *Burning Small Fires* (a documentation of the burning of an Ed Ruscha book). Probably the rarest item I've seen here was a copy of the Marcel Duchamp publication known as the *Green Box*. The signature was almost faded, but all the pieces were there and intact, and there were even a couple of scrap papers with original notes in Duchamp's handwriting—a shopping list and a sort of to-do list by the maestro himself, making this item totally unique.

What's the go-to book you recommend your customers give someone as a gift?

Vanishing Point: How to Disappear in America Without a Trace. It's a tract drawn from survivalists and right-wing libertarians, but also anarchists and left-wing militants, on living off the grid. Useful in this day and age, with instructions on how to syphon gasoline and fake your own death. We have versions by Seth Price and Susanne Bürner.

What is the most gratifying part of your job? What are the greatest challenges of the job?

The look on a visitor's face when they "get it," that these are not conventional art books, but actual works of art in book form. Also, reviewing consignment statements and signing consignment checks—a ton of the books we carry are consigned by independent artists, publishers, and small presses; supporting them and the vital work they do is what Printed Matter is all about.

Who is the most famous customer you have ever had in your shop?

I'd rather not say, but we have our fair share of celebrity visitors. I suppose most are more in the art world or "subculture" vein. My best celebrity Printed Matter sighting by far was in the mid-1990s, when we saw this big guy, surrounded by an entourage, pulling a couple of suitcases out of the trunk of this big black limousine right outside the window. It was Muhammad Ali, and when he looked up and saw me and a couple of fellow workers gawking at him, he gave us a little nod and a smile—it was like a religious experience. We found out later that he was delivering material from his archive to a production studio across the street that was working on a documentary film about him.

What is the weirdest question you have ever been asked at the shop?

My brother-in-law used to phone prank us by identifying himself as a dead contemporary artist whenever he would call for me—kind of macabre, produced some giggles, but more so confusion.

Tell me a bit about the New York and the Los Angeles Art Book Fairs. What was the inspiration behind starting them?

Printed Matter had been a cofounder and coproducer of the Editions/Artists' Books Fair since the late 1990s. It was slanting more toward editions and we—myself and then Printed Matter's director, A. A. Bronson—felt there was a need for a fair that was just focused on artists' books and other art books. The E/AB Fair is a wonderful enterprise that continues to this day, run by the Lower East Side Printshop, but the growth and success of Printed Matter's New York and Los Angeles Art Book Fairs is clear evidence that there really was a need for an art and artists' book-focused fair. The fairs were the brainchild of A. A. Bronson, who founded and developed them. The late Shannon Michael Cane stewarded them to a new scope and level.

What is the greatest enemy of the publishing world?

Corporate monopoly capitalism, essentially everyone's (including the capitalists') greatest enemy.

What do you think the publishing industry needs for support? How do you envision the future of bookshops and the publishing world?

I can't really speak to the publishing industry, but more to the art and artists' publishing community, and even more specifically to the artists' book publishing community. That community needs more public exposure, and ways to reach beyond art-oriented audiences. Printed Matter's fairs, and the many other art book fairs that are happening across the globe—many inspired by and modeled after Printed Matter's fairs—are terrific ways to do this. We also need to cultivate new generations of collectors—if artists' books are the art form you're collecting, you can become a collector with a very modest budget. People need to understand that artists' book collecting is a totally valid form of art collecting, and that the purchase of the book is, in a way, a part of the artwork's concept, because artists' books are about an alternative and independent economy of cultural production and distribution.

If you could change something in the publishing or bookselling industry, what would it be?
Outlaw corporate capitalist monopolies. A vast majority of everything published in the world falls under the umbrella of huge information, media, and entertainment conglomerates, and most of it is true garbage.

If you wrote a book, where would you set it in New York? What street would the main character live on?
I wouldn't write a book, I would create an artist's book. It might or might not have characters . . . And if so, they would live on the page.

What's the best place to sit down and read in the city?
For me, it's in my East Village apartment.

Aside from Printed Matter, what is the best bookshop in the city?
Printed Matter Saint Mark's, our first-time satellite store on Second Avenue and Saint Mark's in the lobby of the Swiss Institute! It's about a tenth of the size of our main space in West Chelsea, but we've packed more than a thousand titles in it, so there's tons to discover and explore. And if you're visiting the East Village, you can stop by Karma Books and the new expanded Mast—it's becoming an art book destination neighborhood!

If you had to repaint Printed Matter a new fun color, what would it be?
We went from black-on-white branding to fluorescent orange and then pink, and now back to black and white. Printed Matter Saint Mark's is black and red (read: anarchists, communists, punk, and Barbara Kruger). I'm fine with the current colors.

If you had to bring only one book with you to a desert island, which would it be?
The biggest encyclopedia available.

According to you, what's the best way to enjoy reading a good book?
For artists' books, just discover, explore, and enjoy them in the context of your everyday life—that's the whole thing. You don't need to go to a museum or a gallery or other cultural destination, you experience the art in book form wherever you may be.

MIDTOWN

New York Public Library

For many visitors, Midtown is New York. Its traffic-choked streets and sidewalks brim with around-the-clock action, its fabled skyline is second to none, and it remains home to some of the city's most iconic landmarks and entertainment. Like much of the island, Midtown has undergone an identity shift, enduring remarkable change while still clinging to the vestiges of its past. Times Square's strip clubs, porn theaters, and pawn shops have long been extinguished, replaced by roving packs of costumed superheroes and big-brand restaurants imported from the rest of America. But the Theater District continues to boom, with patrons feasting at Sardi's before heading off to a Broadway show or jazz club. Book-lovers might decide to choose an alcohol-infused off-Broadway production at the Drunk Shakespeare theater.

Along the Avenue of the Americas, throngs of walkers jockey to catch a glimpse of *Good Morning America* filming, or cautiously skate the ice at Rockefeller Center. From Thanksgiving to New Year's Eve, the entire stretch is transformed into a holiday wonderland, where guests pay homage to the towering Christmas tree before snacking on roasted nuts and heading to the festive window displays outside Bergdorf's and Tiffany's on Fifth Avenue.

From Midtown West, anchored by Madison Square Garden and the glorious James A. Farley Post Office, to Midtown East, where the United Nations headquarters hangs on the East River, visitors will find a region steeped in America's grandest architecture. Notable favorites include the Empire State Building, the Chrysler Building, the stunning Grand Central Station (please go to the Grand Central Oyster Bar) and, of course, my personal obsession, the New York Public Library's incredible main branch. Five blocks north of the library was home up until 2007 to Gotham Book Mart—this world renowned destination was more than just a bookstore, people used to refer to it as a literary salon. Even Truman Capote found solace in Midtown, when he resided at 860 United Nations Plaza in Turtle Bay, where he purchased a twenty-third-floor apartment with the royalties he earned from *In Cold Blood*.

The Morgan Library & Museum
225 Madison Avenue

Along with the main branch of the New York Public Library, some of the city's most important museums, Central Park, and a few other notable landmarks, the Morgan Library & Museum is one of New York's most wonderful destinations. While this statement would be true irrespective of whether or not someone is a bibliophile, the Morgan Library & Museum is without a doubt the most stunning and impressive site a true booklover could possibly pay a visit to on a literary tour of New York.

Originally the private library of one of America's most notable financiers, Pierpont Morgan (of J. P. Morgan & Company), the 1906 neoclassical structure was built by Charles McKim as a place to house Morgan's literary and artistic acquisitions, and was adjacent to his residence on 36th Street and Madison Avenue. Pierpont's collection and interests were known to be encyclopedic—he acquired precious items in practically all mediums, from drawings to prints, ancient objects, and, of course, rare books and manuscripts. It was not until 1924 that Pierpont's son, J. P. Morgan, Jr. (known as Jack), donated the Morgan Library to the public, in what has been called one of the most momentous cultural gifts in U.S. history.

Today, whether for a tourist or a local, the Morgan Library & Museum is available for epic and memorable visits every day, except for Mondays. Admission is steep, but the visit is well worth the price: Mr. Morgan's library, his study, and the rotunda alone are truly unforgettable rooms, each of which would warrant their own daylong visits if time allowed. The Museum, however, is vast, and was actually developed as a "campus" of sorts over the past few decades. Its latest expansion by the great Italian architect Renzo Piano added a significant seventy-five thousand square feet to the whole place.

The Morgan hosts a variety of unique and recurring events—from weekly concerts on the lower level to the seasonal apparition of our dear friend Ebenezer Scrooge during the annual *A Christmas Carol* exhibition. Furthermore, the campus is also equipped with all sorts of joyful things, such as Sol LeWitt's *Wall Drawing 552D*, or, more pertinently to the literary visitor, the famous Reading Room—a true paradise for researchers in need of rare materials on history, art, and literature of the Western world, among many other topics.

To try to depict the extraordinary emotions and literary senses the Morgan awakens in most of its visitors in a simple one-page description would be sinful—similar, perhaps, to an attempt at grasping the idea of what seeing the precious pieces of paper held together on Mr. Morgan's shelves might be like. So on that note, I would advise you to look to the left, make note of the Morgan Library & Museum's address, and run over there as soon as humanly possible.

The Library Hotel
299 Madison Avenue (at East 41st Street)

Could you think of anything more delightful for a booklover than to stay in a library-themed hotel? Located exactly on Library Way in the epicenter of Midtown Manhattan—a block east from the main branch of the New York Public Library—the Library Hotel is a real treat for any book-obsessed explorer. It is actually part of a chain called the Library Hotel Collection—A Novel Approach to Hospitality ("novel," like a book—get it?), with hotels in New York, Toronto, Budapest, and Prague, but this particular one in Midtown is the most library-like of them all. Each floor is devoted to one of the categories of the Dewey Decimal system, rooms are filled with books or "literary-inspired" art, and there is also an actual "reading room" on the second floor where you can get refreshments . . . or books! I don't usually love themed hotels because I find them a bit tacky; but I do just fall for anything book related. And if you're a local and don't need a place to crash, there's also a charming rooftop bar with a suitable bibliophile's view of the library standing regally over Bryant Park.

The Drama Book Shop
Midtown West—"off Broadway..."

After celebrating a whole century of existence, nearly two decades of which were in its West 40th Street location, the Drama Book Shop—a home and refuge for actors, directors, producers, or simply theater lovers of New York—closed its doors in early 2019. However, the happy ending to this dramatic story is that Lin-Manuel Miranda, the homegrown star behind the blockbuster Broadway hit *Hamilton*, and some of his castmates and colleagues, purchased the store to save it from extinction. As early as fall 2019, a brand-new Drama Book Shop is scheduled to reopen, still in the Midtown area, and in the vicinity of theaters, where it truly belongs. As it has always been, the Drama Book Shop will continue to be a hub for performing artists and drama fans. Like its predecessor, the new space is expected to have a small theater—remember the basement of West 40th Street, where Miranda had in fact written *In the Heights*, sitting at the piano? Hopefully, its stock will be replenished, so that once again the shop will have the biggest inventory of play scripts ever gathered in one place. The new store will also be filled with all sorts of books, from plays themselves to screenplays, guides to dramatic writing, and books of advice on how to go for a good casting interview—as well as all kinds of theatrical toys, gadgets, mugs, totes, and tees bearing the shop's cool logo.

The new location will apparently be even bigger than the previous one, which was already spacious and pleasant enough. As the proud recipient of a Tony Honor for Excellence in the Theater, we hope the shop will celebrate its bicentennial in its new space. The Drama Book Shop was everything one could dream of: friendly, cheerful, charming, and charismatic—all in all, a very theatrical experience.

The New York Public Library Main Branch
476 Fifth Avenue

Majestically guarded by Patience and Fortitude, the main branch of the New York Public Library, Astor, Lenox and Tilden Foundations sits adjacent to Bryant Park on the corner of Fifth Avenue and 42nd Street, on what used to be the Croton Reservoir. Patience and Fortitude are the two lions made of pink Tennessee marble (by Edward Clark Potter and the Piccirilli Brothers, and produced for a total cost of thirteen thousand dollars) who have been watching over Fifth Avenue since 1912, protecting the very grand Carrere & Hastings' Beaux-Arts building. Baptized by Mayor Fiorello LaGuardia in the 1930s, Patience (the lion who sits to the south and who was also known prior as Leo Astor and then Lady Astor) and Fortitude (the lion to the north, previously named Leo Lenox, then Lord Lenox) were the two qualities the mayor deemed New Yorkers would need during the economic depression. These wise names have stuck and haven't been changed since.

The atmosphere as you walk in the main doors up the majestic stairs on Fifth Avenue—or even if you decide to enter through the discreet side entrance at 42nd Street—is second to none. Part intimidating and part impressive, the feeling of these giant palatial museum-like hallways is glorious, lavish, and monumental. Feel free to step in for a quick wander, a more in-depth (guided if you wish) tour, or a visit to its numerous and frequent exhibits. Or if, like me, you are really keen, pick one of the many stately reading rooms to study and meditate in. The Rose Main Reading Room, with its celebrated vaulted ceiling and windows looking out over Bryant Park, is what this library is most famous for; but I personally much enjoy the DeWitt Wallace Periodical Room, whose wood-paneled walls bear murals depicting some of the city's most famous buildings with connections to the world of literature.

When Governor Samuel J. Tilden (who lived in what is now the National Arts Club on Gramercy Park South) died in 1886, he left most of his fortune (approximately $2.4 million, after some unfortunate family contestations) to establish and maintain a free library and reading room in the city of New York. At the time, there were already two libraries in New York. Though they did not completely operate the way public libraries do now, they provided New Yorkers with books and material for research.

Founded in 1849, the Astor Library was right below today's Astor Place in what is now the New York Shakespeare Festival's Joseph Papp Public Theater. At the end of the nineteenth century, that area was widely established as Book Row, housing more than forty-eight bookstores along Fourth Avenue, from there to Union Square.

There was also the Lenox Library, originally started in James Lenox's home, which was not too far from Book Row, at Fifth Avenue and 12th Street. Lenox collected art and lots of books, which he would have bound and then let pile up around his house. When it got too messy, he decided to move the collection and commissioned

Richard Morris Hunt in 1870 to design what was considered one of the greatest architectural works in New York at the time. The Gilded Age masterpiece cost over half a million to build, and another half for the land. The Lenox Library was an intellectual landmark, and hosted the very first Gutenberg Bible to ever cross the Atlantic. However, following Lenox's death in 1880, the library's finances started to deteriorate. In 1912, shortly after the Fifth Avenue library's foundation, it was destroyed and replaced by what is now known as the Frick Collection.

It was on May 23, 1895, that the creation of the New York Public Library was made official thanks to John Bigelow, a New York attorney and Tilden trustee, who wrote up a plan that was hailed as an unprecedented act of philanthropy. The library's director was Dr. John Shaw Billings, known as one of the most brilliant librarians of his time. It took sixteen years to finalize everything: Billings's master plan, which was first drawn on a scrap of paper; consolidation with the New York Free Circulating Library in 1901; Carnegie's $5.2 million investment; and the acquisition of more than a million books for the Fifth Avenue branch to open officially to the public on May 24, 1911.

At 9:08 a.m., one of the first library patrons filed a slip for N. IA. Grot's *Nravstvennye idealy nashego vremeni* (*Ethical Ideas of Our Time*), a study of Friedrich Nietzsche and Leo Tolstoi. The book was delivered six minutes later. That day, between thirty- and fifty-thousand people paid a visit to the new library, which is still to this day a major intellectual institution and an essential part of New York.

Whether you are a longtime New York resident or a first-time visitor, no New York experience would be complete without an exploration of this library branch's halls—or even just a quick hello to Patience and Fortitude. And, one cannot disregard the fact that one of this iconic library's treasures is Columbus's 1493 letter announcing his discovery of the New World. You can find that in the Rare Book Division, on the third floor of the building.

Christopher J. Platt

Chief Branch Library Officer
for The New York Public Library

The New York Public Library's mission is to "inspire lifelong learning, advance knowledge, and strengthen our communities." Would you say the NYPL achieves that? How has it evolved since its opening more than a century ago?

I would say it achieves its mission every day—even though every new day is always a challenge to achieve it. But it is core to what we do, and what we have done since we opened over a hundred years ago, and how we have grown over the time.

I would say what has evolved is how we achieve it. We have done that by opening new spaces. For example, the Mulberry Street Library, where you like to work, is one of our new spaces, whereas for Jefferson Market, we took over the building (which was from the 1800s) in the 1960s.

The formats that we deliver have changed, of course. Books are constant, thank God. But it was really controversial when we started putting paperbacks in our collections in the late 1960s. Then we also started putting audio books, and that went from LPs to cassette tapes to audio CDs. And now we are offering online and streaming media that is really popular with our libraries. So how we deliver it is changing.

The other thing I would say is in the last decade or so, the library is focused on using those community spaces—those community libraries that we have in eighty-eight locations across our service area—to be more explicit centers of learning and centers of gathering for the community. We have increased the number of children's programs that we offer, as well as how we offer them, so that we are more deliberate to promote the act of reading and the importance of reading, not just to the children but also to their parents and caregivers or educators who accompany them. This is all hugely important to us, and it is also important to the city in which we serve—it aligns with the mayor's priorities and the Department of Education's priorities as well. We want to make sure we are building the next generation of readers, because inspiring lifelong learning, advancing knowledge, and strengthening the communities—you really need the core foundational things in place to do that, and reading is one activity that hits all of those core things.

In the last two years, we have been zeroing in with laser focus on this. Our mantra within the library is "more people reading more," which sounds simplistic when you say it out loud—but "more people" is about reaching new people. We are a city of immigrants, a city that is a challenge to live in, and many people who come here don't understand what that local public library on the corner is, or whether they are even welcome in it and what we can offer to them. So we are really looking at how we can reach out and build out to new communities, which is stuff we have done for the past hundred years. And then reading more, which I mentioned. We have really upped our programming, and also if you walk into the libraries, you can see new ways in which libraries are promoting reading, and reading as an activity. Our partnerships with "One Book, One New York," or with the mayor's office, or with HBO (#ReadingIsLit)—these are recent things, which illustrate how we see reading as an activity that really needs to be promoted, and we have a responsibility and an opportunity because we are in every community to help foster that.

Would you say that in certain communities—where the demographics have changed over the past years—the libraries and the resources they offer have evolved with those demographics and the community?
Absolutely. The goal of the library is always to be one step ahead where we can. But absolutely, we change with our communities.

Chinatown is a really great example. The Chatham Square Library on East Broadway was one of the original Carnegie Libraries. When it first opened, it was a typical early-1900s Lower East Side community library that was very Jewish, with a lot of Yiddish and Hebrew books. Over the years, with the 1950s civil rights movement, new immigration acts were signed and the population of Chinese users grew, and that library has become a center for Chinese reading and Chinese heritage for that community, and has been for a very long time now. Similarly, the Seward Park Library up the street has also evolved. It still has a remnant of the old Hebrew and Yiddish and Jewish collections that used to be in both locations, but now when you walk into the Chatham Square Library, nine out of ten people who walk through those doors are of non-English-speaking background.

More recently, if you go up to the Parkchester Library in the Bronx—there is a growing Bengali community in the Parkchester and Westchester Square areas—you'll find we have worked very hard to build the Bengali and other Hindi languages selection in those libraries for people to come in and read.

We are lucky in New York, because readers will read just about anything. James Patterson is popular everywhere, but sometimes the reader in Fort Washington wants to read James Patterson in Russian or the reader in Parkchester wants to read him in Bengali, so that is how we try to help them out.

What do you see in the the New York Public Library's future? Will it grow or stay the same?
That is the million-, or even the billion-dollar question. We talk about it all the time. The one thing I will say, and which we are all absolutely confident about, is that the library will still be here and the library will still be the largest circulating public library in the USA and be serving one of the most vibrant, urban centers on the planet. But how we do that and where we grow strategically will affect what it looks like going forward.

We are still building and renovating branches. We have opened probably half a dozen branches in the last decade. We have a completely new branch being opened in the Charleston section of Staten Island, which is way south near New Jersey, in a couple of years. So the spaces themselves are still important to people. People still really see the local library as a civic entity that they want to help define their communities with.

But we are still growing in other ways. Digital is one obvious area where we are doing a lot of investment, and I would say a lot of what you see on our website or simply with our eBook reading app are things we didn't have ten years ago and that we are going to continue to grow. These are not so visible to the naked eye, unless you are looking at it through a screen to see the array of what is there, but it is massive and important. That is probably the area of the library that will grow the most going forward. We have a massive digital images collection, one of the largest in the world. A lot of the archives and papers that the research centers collect, we are also wondering how to promote digitally going forward. Increasingly also, as we acquire new collections, they have digital imprints that we gather, too.

Do you have a lot of secret sections in certain libraries?
There are a lot of hidden nooks and crannies, especially in the Schwarzman library, up here at 42nd Street. The secret sections that are still left in libraries, which everybody talks about, are only few: the old custodial apartments, for example. The Carnegie Libraries were all built with a custodian, who would live in the library with their family to help keep the boiler running all day. Many of the Carnegie Libraries still have remnants of an apartment above, but those are being changed into public spaces. The last custodial apartment was occupied in the late 1990s, believe it or not, but we have been actively changing the places around into public spaces. Our Washington Heights library, Epiphany, Chatham Square, Tompkins Square—all of their old custodial apartments have been changed into program spaces that the staff use for story time or adult book discussions. If you are going up to the third floor, typically you are walking into an old custodial apartment.

Are there any lesser-known New York Public Library branches that are must-sees and that people don't necessarily know about?
Yes, I am glad you asked. Mulberry Street in itself is this kind of fun little hidden gem in that old converted chocolate factory, and you walk in and have to go down instead of up. Another one I love

to tell people about is the Ottendorfer Library, off of Saint Marks. It is the oldest operating public library building in the city, and has so much history from when that neighborhood was a German neighborhood. It is so rich in history. Another library I like to tell people about is the Tottenville Library on the very southern tip of Staten Island, which is a gem of an original Carnegie Library. It is like stepping back in time. It has a gracious front lawn with big, beautiful shade trees, and you are in this little village. You think you are miles and miles away from the city, which you are. It is great. City Island Library in the Bronx (which, incidentally, has some great seafood places) is isolated and has a small nautical collection. In fact, people who are just boating up and down the island will sometimes stop and use the nautical collection to learn how to fix their boats. The Macomb's Bridge Library in one of the original housing projects in Harlem is another one I love. It is the size of a studio apartment. In terms of its programming, compared to the other eighty-seven libraries, inch for inch, it does more programming than any other branch. This is not because it is so small, but because it so extensively used. In the summer, we overflow their programming into the courtyard outside because so many people attend. If we are lucky, we may be able to move them into a larger space in the next couple of years. It is a little vibrant showhouse to what a library can mean to a local community. And Terence Cardinal Cooke-Cathedral Library is a small branch we have in a subway stop, underground off of Lexington Avenue.

Reading Room
at Bryant Park
Bryant Park

From about 1935 to 1944, the New York Public Library provided New Yorkers with what they called an "Open Air Library." Its mission was to give "out-of-work businessmen and intellectuals a place to go" during the Depression Era. No money, no library card or ID, and no address were needed to enjoy the books this out-of-the-ordinary library was offering. It closed after World War II, once people started getting jobs again.

In 2003, HSBC and Bryant Park revived the Open Air Library and created the Reading Room, which in turn offers books, newspapers, and magazines for free usage from April to October, when the weather is nice. If it rains, there is usually a tent set up or an alternative location for their events, if necessary. Those literary events include children's story time and activities, author appearances and lectures, and a world-class poetry program. The Reading Room is located in Bryant Park, right behind the New York Public Library's main branch, and features custom-designed carts full of books, children's stuff, and all sorts of reading material. It makes for a great and original combination of an outdoor library and a creative, literary playground—and provides invaluable reading matter for lunching Midtowners.

The Round Table
at the Algonquin Hotel
59 West 44th Street

The Algonquin is quite a nice hotel—actually qualified as the luxury variety—located in Midtown Manhattan. A tourist's favorite, it's situated within walking distance of several of Midtown's chief attractions in Grand Central, Bryant Park, and Times Square. What sets this hotel apart are two things: it has been designated as a New York City Historic Landmark; and, more importantly, it is home to what is known as the Algonquin Round Table.

Right after World War I, a group of rather intelligent and witty twenty-something New York writers, critics, and actors, who nicknamed themselves "The Vicious Circle," started meeting for lunch at the Algonquin on a daily basis. The hotel was only a few doors from the offices of *Vanity Fair*, where Dorothy Parker, Robert Benchley, and Robert E. Sherwood worked. One of their first meetings was a luncheon to which the theater agent John Peter Toohey invited Alexander Woollcott (*New York Times* drama critic), for a special welcome back from the war, where he had been sent to write for *Stars and Stripes*. Toohey's initial intention was to lay into Woollcott, who had refused to write about one of Toohey's clients, Eugene O'Neill—but the luncheon ended up being very jolly, and the first of many more to follow.

The Round Table became famous for the ideas and gossip exchanged by the various critics and writers in attendance. Some of those included George S. Kaufman, Heywood Broun, Edna Ferber, and Marc Connelly, among many others. They influenced authors like Fitzgerald and Hemingway, and it is said that the funding to create the *New Yorker* in 1925 was secured by Harold Ross at one of these gatherings. To this day, a copy of the magazine can still be found in each room.

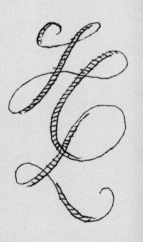

For the past eighty years, the Round Table has been celebrating literary brilliance, and claims to have been "serving New York's literary, artistic, and theatrical elite." Today, the Round Table offers a fine dining experience and "still inspires with a tasteful and modern take on American cuisine"—while its true cultural legacy lives on in all of our minds.

Book Off
49 West 45th Street

I love the Book Off logo because it instantly makes you feel like you are in Japan. Book Off is the biggest Japanese chain selling secondhand items such as books, comics, and CDs, among other things—and who doesn't love all of that?

There is a very exciting 1990s feel to Book Off, which is reminiscent of my first discovery of Japan and my first full enjoyment of buying secondhand books and music for (very) cheap. Almost like a cross between an old-school Virgin Megastore and a genuine indoor flea market, the New York Book Off branch is a fun destination. Without quite being like Japan, it is still a megastore of sorts, where you will be able to get your fix of manga, books, music, magazines, and whatnot for as low as one dollar. Also, if you decide you do not want them anymore and would rather sell them back, you can do that, too.

Japan Society
333 East 47th Street

For the past 111 years, the Japan Society has been committed to deepening mutual understanding between the United States and Japan. As a huge Japanophile, I could not help but be intrigued by this nonprofit organization that sits deep in Midtown East and offers interesting cultural and linguistic programming year-round—and quite a wealth of historical background, too.

Currently located on 47th Street by the East River, in what was once known as the Japan House, the Society offers film screenings, lectures, and workshops. Designed by the modernist architect Junzo Yoshimura, the extraordinary building opened to the public in September 1971. It is now one of the youngest landmarked buildings in New York. Crossing over the street from Dag Hammarskjöld Plaza—and as a side note, there is also a Dag Hammarskjöld Library (the UN Library) which is sadly not open to the general public—the entrance gives a feeling of stepping directly into Japan.

Down in the building's language center, you will find a secluded and quiet little library. A very small room filled with Japanese books provides serenity and a calming literary retreat for language students or simple passersby—who, in fact, need to ask the chief librarian for permission to visit, which is usually granted. The floor is carpeted and there is a distinct 1970s atmosphere within the room, which makes it all very comforting and comfortable. A pleasant little break from the hustle and bustle of the busy Midtown UN area and the neighboring FDR Drive.

Drunk Shakespeare
777 Eighth Avenue

New York will never cease to amaze me—which is why I recently found myself purchasing vouchers for the first play I have been to in about a quarter century. As a person who is formally opposed to any theater outing except for movie theaters (and I tend to doze off, if it is not an action film or a rom-com), I have not been to see a play or the ballet or the opera, or any performance really, since I was a child. My maternal grandmother used to force me to attend such things; now though, as an adult, she no longer has such sway over me.

My husband, always wanting to go to Broadway—or even off Broadway, or even Lincoln Center, or even anything—was a bit taken aback. Upon announcing to him that we were finally going to the theater, he did not expect me to reveal it was for something titled "Drunk Shakespeare." He accepted to go because he is nice. I accepted to go (besides the fact that I'd bought the tickets already) because of two things I like: books and (sometimes) getting drunk.

Set in the center of a room organized as a library full of color-coordinated books (I know, don't start), five actors proceed to perform a Shakespeare play of their choosing in an intimate closed-set type of atmosphere. And the punchline/main event/most fun/greatest attraction of this all is that the main actor performing has to drink five shots of whiskey. During the play, spectators can also order drinks, snacks, and whatever else they fancy. There is an ever so slight and inoffensive level of engagement from the public, too—meaning that if you somehow wish to participate a bit, you can.

We saw *Macbeth*, and a charming actress named Aubrey was the drunk performer—we went to a late-night 10 p.m. performance, so she had actually had about a dozen shots by the end of it, but she was surprisingly good and agile. I did not expect this at all, but the participatory aspect of the performance was what I liked the most. Not a literary landmark per se, but this is something different, and perhaps, in its unexpected and gentle rowdiness, more reminiscent of Shakespearean times than our literature professors would have us think.

Instituto Cervantes
211 East 49th Street

Hidden among some of Midtown East's most densely office-filled streets is a secret garden, surrounded by a few buildings that constitute a center and library dedicated to Spanish culture: the Instituto Cervantes. I spent at least two years or so walking down 49th Street from east to west and west to east with a very dear friend without ever noticing anything fishy. On our latest visit to that street, we saw a small bright red sign fixed to the wall. It read Instituto Cervantes at Amster Yard, a NYC Landmark since 1966.

Indeed, "the Amster Yard was said to have been the terminal stop of the Boston Stage Coach on the Eastern Post Road"—another historical tidbit you can read on an old plaque on the wall once you walk through the Spanish Center's easily missed gate. A bonus fact that caught my attention was that Amster Yard also served as the great sculptor Isamu Noguchi's residence at some point.

We found out there was also a whole controversy surrounding the installation of the institute some fifteen years ago, when some of the landmarked buildings were destroyed without permission. Thankfully, the garden courtyard remains as charming as ever, and if you need to improve (or even get started on) your knowledge of Spanish, this might be just the right place for you.

The center is actually affiliated with a bigger organization with head-quarters in Madrid and with the goal of promoting the Spanish language and spreading Spanish and Hispanic-American culture. The center's New York Jorge Luis Borges Library houses approximately eighty-five thousand items in various formats. And if, like me, you speak zero Spanish and just fancy a read in a remote little library or a sit-down in a beautiful secluded courtyard, that's also okay.

Terence Cardinal Cooke-Cathedral Library
560 Lexington Avenue

Have you ever been to a library in a subway station? The Terence Cardinal Cooke-Cathedral Library (previously part of the New York Archdiocese's Cathedral Library Association when it was founded in 1887) is located on the northeast corner of Lexington Avenue and 50th Street. It is right below ground, in between street level and the Lexington Avenue/53rd Street station, which serves the E, M, and 6 trains. Nobody really knows about this microscopic secret hideout. I did not, until the chief branch library officer told me about it; in fact, nor did the unfriendly woman who was working at the subway station. She had no clue what I was talking about. But to be honest, when spoken out loud, asking if there was a library in a subway station did sound a bit surreal.

Very neighborhood-feeling, the Terence Cardinal Cooke-Cathedral Library reminded me of a smaller version of the local Swiss Cottage Library in London that I used to go to with my grandmother as a child. It is cozy, sweet, and has the basic necessities a library needs. A definite must if you are in search of a special library experience like no other, and if you need a calming little read in the middle of busy and bustling Lexington Avenue.

53rd Street Library
18 West 53rd Street

The new library at West 53rd Street, right off of Fifth Avenue and sitting glamorously across the street from the MoMA (with which it will be hosting events and programs) offers, in my opinion, exactly what is needed of a library on summer Sundays, when Patience and Fortitude's main branch decides to take a break.

Baptized an "amphitheater laptop bar" by David Dunlap in the *New York Times*, this particular branch has drawn wide criticism. I must concur that the lack of books in this modernized and comfortable basement full of technological facilities is indeed quite striking. The true gripe for New Yorkers was probably more to do with the eight years of library-free life this pocket of the city endured starting in 2008, when the famed and beloved Donnell Library Center closed and was replaced by an ugly fifty-story luxury condominium. According to the *New York Times*, the term "luxury" hardly suffices, since one of the apartments in that new building sold for a figure just south of twenty-three million dollars—and funnily enough, twenty-three million dollars was the sum it cost to build this new library, which is entirely subterranean.

What it lacks in architectural charm, it compensates for in its abundance of modern facilities, its wealth of resources, and the same cast of likable characters you're likely to find in other New York libraries. To guard such facilities and keep an eye on such characters, they seem to have invested in a very efficient security team, constantly patrolling the grounds, asking anybody who is not reading a book, flicking through a pamphlet, or staring at a screen if they are "okay."

The library's convenient layout lends itself to conventional and very concentrated workers (like myself—when I am not busy observing my colleagues), younger students in workout gear, and random neighborhood visitors. One feature of this library I have taken a particular liking to is the fact that, after sinking into the depths of its basement levels, cellphone reception is not optimal.

The Museum of Modern Art Library
4 West 54th Street

If you enter the lesser-known Lewis B. and Dorothy Cullman Education and Research Building, one door over from the back entrance of the Museum of Modern Art on 54th Street, you will be faced with a rather official structure guarded by a friendly man. To the right, through huge windows, the Abby Aldrich Rockefeller Sculpture Garden, with its bar, restaurant, and loving crowd, is still visible. The cool and memorable MoMA logos and typography are all over most of the building, making it clear that you are still within a museum affiliation and an extension of its premises. On the upper floors of this building, you will find the official MoMA Library, as well as its Archives, among many other institutional treasures.

With a collection devoted to modern and contemporary art, this non-circulating library comprises more than three-hundred thousand volumes full of information about painting, sculpture, drawings, photography, prints, design, architecture, film, video, performance, and emerging art forms from the late nineteenth century to today. The library is open to the public, although an appointment is necessary, and it most specifically caters to researchers studying modern and contemporary art, architecture, design, and emerging art forms. There is also a Circulating Film and Video Library near MoMA's PS1 outpost in Long Island City.

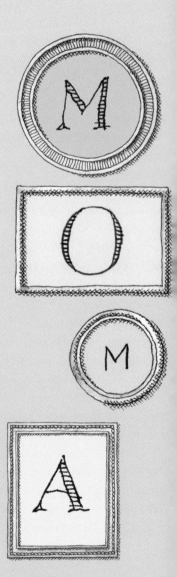

The Plaza
Fifth Avenue at Central Park South

The Plaza is not only one of the grandest hotels in New York; it also happens to be the setting for the famous quarrel between Tom and Gatsby in *The Great Gatsby*. When the whole gang drives to New York, they get a suite at the hotel; Tom confronts Gatsby about Daisy; and, in case some of you have not read Fitzgerald's succulent master-piece, I shall stop right here.

Another one of New York's essential literary figures also has a connection to the Plaza: Truman Capote. On November 28, 1966, Capote threw what the *New York Times* dubbed "the best party ever" in the Grand Ballroom of the Plaza. More than five hundred of his most fancy, glamorous, and literary friends were in attendance—all dressed in black and white.

A historical New York landmark, the Plaza was also once known as a place where "nothing unimportant ever happens." For me, the Plaza is also home to one of my childhood (and adulthood, come to think of it) favorite literary heroines . . . One of my constant internal debates is whether I prefer Eloise or Madeline. But why must I choose? It should not be a debate. It should be love in equal measures—as it is meant to be with your parents, or your children. When I assess the situation though, I realize I have as many different volumes for each one of them in my son's room—*Eloise* (the original), *Eloise in Paris*, *Eloise in Moscow*, and *Eloise at Christmastime*; versus *Madeline* (the original), *Madeline's Christmas*, *Madeline's Rescue*, *Madeline in London*. See—the numbers are equal.

What could be better than spending a weekend staying in the Eloise Suite, rereading *The Great Gatsby*, and letting your imagination flow? The Eloise Suite at the Plaza is also all pink and mostly covered in little Eloises. To add to the excitement, it was decorated by the iconic fashion designer Betsey Johnson. You could also take your child to get an Eloise root beer float or some scones served on Eloise-themed tableware. Alternatively, you can also probably buy the tableware and an array of toys, gifts, clothing, and books from the Eloise gift shop on the concourse level of the hotel.

One more cute idea would be to host an Eloise birthday party for kids—or, if nobody has a birthday yet, there are all sorts of Eloise events at the hotel to attend year-round. And if, like me, you are an adult and cannot attend such events, you could just go to the Plaza, sit in the Palm Court, order an alcoholic beverage, and pretend to be Daisy Buchanan—or an adult version of Eloise; that works too.

Argosy Book Store
116 East 59th Street

Argosy Book Store is officially the oldest bookshop in New York City. Currently in its third generation of family ownership, Argosy first opened its doors in 1925 as one of the staples on Book Row (on 4th Avenue downtown, where Alabaster Books now stands alone). Now occupying a moderately tall building on 59th Street, slightly west of Lexington Avenue, Argosy has much to offer on four different levels.

The first floor feels quite fancy and a bit European, with all its leather-bound antique tomes of classic literature and a variety of out-of-print books spanning all types of subjects. The old-school posters and sentimental photographs adorning the walls, and the green carpeted floors, give the place a cozy atmosphere.

Step downstairs and you will feel like you have entered a clandestine Ali Baba cave full of books. Everything you need and much more is available, all classified by topic: philosophy, theater, poetry, fiction (organized alphabetically). The floors in the basement are painted red (no carpet this time) and it truly feels like you have secretly gone down to your uncle's forbidden cave to try to find treasures. And treasures you will find. It is easy to get lost and spend too much time down there, as you do really feel transported. That strange otherworldly feeling is quite relaxing in its own way.

Go back upstairs and take the elevator (operated by a charming young man, who won't unnecessarily engage in small talk) to the fifth floor. Up there are all sorts of books, mostly made up of history, and this time organized by region. A nice man guards this floor very efficiently, and will be able to assist you with anything you need. He leaves at about 3:30 p.m., so be sure to get there on the earlier side!

On the second floor, there are maps and prints in a setting that resembles a gallery more than a bookshop. There are also cute little globes for sale. I believe the third and fourth floors are mostly used for storage, though I know a lot of their stock is kept in a warehouse in Brooklyn. This shop is a definite must for any literary journey, as it will soon be celebrating its first century. Here is to many more!

The Sherry-Netherland
781 Fifth Avenue

Located directly across from Central Park, on the very edge of its southeast corner, the stupendous looking Sherry-Netherland replaced the old Hotel New Netherland (built for William Waldorf Astor, great-grandson of John Jacob Astor who left all the money for Astor Library). Erected in 1927 and measuring just north of five hundred and sixty feet tall, it was considered the tallest apartment-hotel in New York at the time it opened.

Today, The Sherry-Netherland is a beautiful cooperative residential hotel with rooms and suites available for short stays as well as luxury apartments for sale. The Sherry-Netherland is a very prestigious Uptown landmark, and is known to have hosted many great intellectual and interesting characters. One of the most notable ones was Ernest Hemingway (the best American author there ever was, in the minds of some), who was famous for staying there whenever he was passing through New York—often on his way to Paris or Venice, or coming from Cuba . . . Hemingway did not seem too fond of New York, and openly made statements about the city, once declaring, "This ain't my town, it's a town you come to for a short time. It's murder."

One time, in 1950, during a visit from his friend Lillian Ross, who wrote a captivating story about the whole trip in the *New Yorker*, Hemingway reportedly requested he receive no visits or calls—except from Miss Dietrich. Upon entering his room, he declared the "joint looks OK" and that it must be "the Chinese Gothic Room." The room had fake books on shelves for decoration and he thus described those as "phony, just like the town." He ordered caviar and Perrier-Jouët brut to the room. A whole slew of events took place in that room, as well as at Abercrombie & Fitch, and at the Metropolitan Museum of Art, among other very New York locations. The room-service dinner with Miss Dietrich was recounted in full detail, as was a whole evening during which she visited her daughter on Third Avenue and cleaned her place with towels from the Plaza while she babysat her grandson. Marlene would catch a cab back to the Plaza, and, having been mistaken for a cleaner by the cab driver, she would shamefully get out a block away from the hotel and walk back . . .

These days, I am not sure whether the same caviar on which the Hemingways, Ms. Ross, and Ms. Dietrich dined is readily available at the Sherry-Netherland, nor if the pasteboard books are still there—but the building, with its lobby ceiling mural recently restored to its original glory in 2014, is still standing, and ravishingly so. The delightful and delicious Harry Cipriani —almost an exact duplicate of the original Harry's Bar in Venice—has its own private door into the hotel, so if you're a hotel guest, easy access to perfect pasta will be no issue.

Tina Brown & Harry Evans

Longtime New York residents and English married couple, and celebrated editors and writers

Harold Evans & Tina Brown

I met with publishing legends Tina Brown CBE (former editor of *Tatler*, *Vanity Fair*, the *New Yorker*, and currently head of Tina Brown Media) and her husband Sir Harold Evans (former editor of the *Sunday Times* and founding editor of *Condé Nast Traveler*) at their new home on the East Side only two weeks after they had moved in.

Brown's and Evans's move from what they casually refer to as 447 (where they hosted countless book launches and parties—so crowded and popular that they had to transfer their own furniture to trucks parked outside) to their charming corner apartment on Beekman Place, involved a severe library downsize from a previously estimated six thousand books to a "mere" two thousand five hundred—at least that was what Brown was aiming for, when editing it all down.

"It was very difficult for me to edit everything," Brown tells me. "We had three categories of books: books that were sent to us by friends, books that were sent to us by publishers, and of course, books that we fancy and love, which we picked ourselves." During the editing process, however, Brown referred to another two categories into which books might fall: "There are all these books I loved reading, which I will never get rid of. If I read something and love it, it immediately becomes a sort of love object that I want to keep and cherish. Then, there are lots of borderline books, like random biographies of photographers—will I ever read this? Is it worth keeping?"

My dad had worked very closely with Evans in the 1980s and early 1990s, when Evans was the editor of *Condé Nast Traveler*. He wrote and illustrated stories in many issues of the magazine. And it was only five minutes before Evans, looking relaxed in his dapper suspenders and pale blue shirt, walked over to one of his *Condé Nast Traveler* bound tomes (the one containing the very first edition from February 1987) to show me pages my dad had illustrated. "This was the very first edition, you see. I'm not sure I can remember where I discovered your father, it was not the *New Yorker*, but I loved his drawings and I let him do whatever he wanted. His style changed a lot over the years, and he did many different things for us." I wanted to ask what my dad was like to work with but we never got to that, as Evans was off to find a copy of his book *The American Century* on another one of his shelves.

I was treated to a grand tour of his personal collection with a particular emphasis on all the books he has about English grammar, which is certainly one of his fields of expertise as well as a true passion. He showed me some of the books he has authored, including his latest work: *Do I Make Myself Clear?: Why Writing Well Matters*. Another subject very close to Evans's heart is typography, and he expressed a clear preference for serif fonts. (I'm confident he will approve of the serif fonts in which the book you are reading now is typset, which are Baskerville and Didot.) He told me about a typeface he designed called Olympia (my sister's name), and extolled the virtues of legibility and intelligent design, before confessing his dislike of the sans serif font used by *Wikipedia*.

Brown is a huge poetry fan and she absolutely loves W. B. Yeats. When I asked her if she reads poetry all in one go like a novel (which in hindsight sounds like an absurd question), she simply referred to the genre as her own form of spiritual sustenance—she reads and rereads it constantly over the years. At one point, she left the room and came back with a beautiful little chest covered in colorful needlepoint. It was filled with all her mother's favorite poetry books that she had left her.

Clearly visible were the endless volumes of bound copies of *Condé Nast Traveler*, the *New Yorker*, *Newsweek*, *Tatler*, and of course, *Vanity Fair*, all arranged meticulously and in chronological order at the bottom of their shelves. The leather-bound tomes were all made at the end of a professional chapter, to keep at home as their personal archive.

The couple walked me through the different areas of the apartment, where both Brown and Evans work—separate nooks in a cozy home office off of the living room. There were shelves and shelves of books: some for work, some for enjoyment. I spotted Virginia Woolf (a favorite of Brown), as well as Evans's top read, Alan Bullock, buried deep in his extensive collection of history books about World War II and the 1930s. There were also many of Brown's social history volumes: books about Cliveden House, Georgiana Spencer, Madame de Sevigne's letters, and diaries of all sorts, among other historical treats.

When I finally asked if the couple ever work together and whether they enjoy it, Brown replied: "Very much so. We work side by side. Harry is my best editor. It's wonderful to work together. We edit each of our pieces. Harry is great on structure, especially if there is no internal logic. I'm good on ideas and style." Evans said: "Tina will cross out the redundancies, the sentences that go on too long, or the adjectives that have been misappropriated." They told me they don't get on each other's toes, and it is usually a harmonious experience. Surely only in the world of literature could two titans of the industry work together so sweetly.

Clubs & Private Libraries in Midtown and Its Environs

The Players Club *16 Gramercy Park South*
The Century Association *7 West 43rd Street*
The General Society of Mechanics & Tradesmen of the City of New York
20 West 44th Street
The Harvard Club of New York City *35 West 44th Street*
The New York Yacht Club *37 West 44th Street*
The Lambs Club *132 West 44th Street*
The Yale Club of New York City *50 Vanderbilt Avenue*
Metropolitan Club *1 East 60th Street*
The Harmonie Club *4 East 60th Street*
The Grolier Club *47 East 60th Street*
Knickerbocker Club *807 Fifth Avenue*
The Colony Club *564 Park Avenue*
The Cosmopolitan Club *122 East 66th Street*
The Explorers Club *46 East 70th Street*

In Midtown, whether you are east or west of Fifth Avenue, you will find there are a few private clubs spread around. Not only do the buildings themselves look absolutely majestic, but I believe their insides are just as glorious. I remember stopping by The Yale Club (which dates from 1897, and is right on the Vanderbilt side of Grand Central) to meet my husband, who was with a journalist (a former Yale student) having a drink at the bar. My Pimm's Cup there was made to perfection—a rarity for a Brit in America—which I found matched the standards of the way the club's bar looked and felt. Sadly, without that journalist friend of my husband's, it is close to impossible for me to penetrate the club. But find yourself a suitably generous member of such an institution, and you're in for a bibliophile's treat. Its library, reasonably sized yet still cozy, seems like it would be ideal to work from—especially if you were coming from somewhere that drops you into Grand Central Station, which of course is also beautiful.

Then there is The Harvard Club, which was founded in 1865. I have never set foot inside, but Jill Abramson, alumnus and booklover, has raved about the place's lovely library—pleasant to read in and full of all sorts of books, and with suitably clubby wood-paneled walls and burgundy leather chairs.

Right next to The Harvard Club, on the same side of West 44th Street, is The New York Yacht Club. While it is typically open only to members and guests, the club offers a monthly visit of the library to anybody who shows interest—so you may be able to try your luck and get a glimpse of a true nautical collection in all its glory. I am fortunate enough to have a friend who's a member, with whom I recently had dinner at the club, and I can most certainly vouch for its impressive library. On a quiet and peaceful upper floor, it is filled with all sorts of nautical treasures, whether they are of the literary genre, travel guides, old reference books, or simply beautiful displays of all the different knots sailors make with rope.

Possibly the most noteworthy of all private clubs for a booklover would be the Grolier Club. A world-famous bibliophile's paradise, the club was founded in 1884 to study and promote the art of book production. It frequently hosts exhibitions, which are open to the public and free.

Other private member-only clubs that have large libraries or interesting book collections include (but are not limited to): The Harmonie Club and Metropolitan Club, both on East 60th Street, and The Century Association on the west side. The Cosmopolitan Club also offers an extremely cozy and elegant library, which appears to be very popular for hosting book clubs, receptions, and events in an intimate setting. There are gender-specific clubs, such as The Colony, a women-only club on Park Avenue and 62nd Street, and The Knickerbocker, which is for men and on the same street but closer to Fifth Avenue. Each has a library or reading room with a renowned and eclectic collection; though I find gender-specific places to be discriminatory in their very nature.

Another club with its own comforting and comfortable library is The Players Club on Gramercy Park. Officially part of The Players Foundation for Theatre Education, the growing collection in this library is made up of books, manuscripts, photographs, prompt books, notebooks, and more than fifty thousand playbills. The collection began with Edwin Booth's personal library.

The Explorers Club has quite a beautiful library with extraordinary resources catering to all kinds of travelers and adventurers. Its material is rather specialized and is usually only available to the Club's members; but if you happen to be a researcher in true need of such material (a bit like Paddington Bear for example), you can make appointments with the curator to visit the library.

On a completely different, and not-too-literary note, there is also The Lambs Club, which used to be the headquarters for The Lambs, America's first professional theatrical group (it still exists), which is a restaurant and bar open to the public. Housed in the same historical building as The Chatwal New York (a hotel), The Lambs Club Restaurant and Bar now offers a modern American menu and classic cocktails in a landmarked building with a storied Broadway past.

It is worth noting that in another type of category (a place that is not a club), there is also the General Society of Mechanics and Tradesmen of the City of New York. Now, this is not a member's club per se, but an active society with a very large library dating back to its founding in 1820—making it the second-oldest library in New York City—which might be of great interest to any booklover. It is absolutely grand and fabulous. And while membership is required for borrowing privileges, the library is open to the public for on-site use. This venerable society also hosts a free lecture series, including book events, details of which they list on their website.

Central Park

Central Park is the fifth largest park in all of New York City, and occupies a very important geographical surface of Manhattan, between the Upper East Side and the Upper West Side. It is the most visited urban park in the United States, and an iconic location for countless famous movies. First established in 1857, the park was landscaped by Frederick Law Olmstead and Calvert Vaux, the latter of whom has already been mentioned in regard to the Tilden Mansion and the Jefferson Market Library.

Central Park is not just important to most New Yorkers for its pleasant green qualities; it is also important to literary heroes. *The Catcher in the Rye*'s Holden Caulfield spends many hours sitting on a bench staring at the pond's ducks, while Grady and Clyde from Truman Capote's first novel, *Summer Crossing*, spend much time at the Central Park Zoo. So even if you are not an outdoor type, you will soon find that Central Park has a lot to offer culturally and prosaically. It is a magical little haven of nature, which is filled with intellectual wonders. And there's even a kiosk of everyone's favorite bookstore—the Strand—on Fifth Avenue and East 60th Street.

The first of these Central Park wonders is the Alice in Wonderland bronze sculpture, in which Alice is surrounded by the Mad Hatter, the White Rabbit, a few mushrooms, and various pets and other characters. Based on the original John Tenniel illustrations from Lewis Carroll's first edition of *Alice's Adventures in Wonderland*, Jose de Creeft's bronze construction was built in 1959. Installed at 74th Street on the East Side of the park, just north of Conservatory Water, people love to take photos with it or just say hello. What's more, you are actually allowed to climb on it and touch it. Who doesn't love Alice—and, more importantly, who doesn't love the White Rabbit?

Head a little north, and you will run into the Delacorte Theater, on the southwest corner of the Great Lawn, just off of 80th Street. This open-air venue, with an 1,872-capacity, is where the Public Theater (whose headquarters are in the former Astor Library landmark downtown) performs its famous Shakespeare in the Park during the summer, as well as many other plays. All performances are free, and make for another interesting way to enjoy your park experience.

Last but not least, all the way up by the Vanderbilt Gate at Fifth Avenue between 104th and 105th streets, is the Conservatory Garden. Divided into three smaller gardens (each with its own Italian, French, or English style), the southern English-style garden encompasses a small water lily pool with two children at one end of it. They depict Mary and Dickon, the main characters from Frances Hodgson Burnett's *The Secret Garden*. The sculptor Bessie Potter Vonnoh paid tribute to everybody's childhood favorite with the Frances Hodgson Burnett Memorial Fountain. Take a little stroll through the Conservatory Garden—and bring a book, since it is designated a "Quiet Zone" by the park.

THE UPPER EAST SIDE

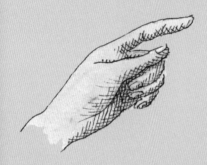

The Upper East Side of Manhattan is fancy, old-school, and quiet. It is filled with lots of classic and beautiful apartment buildings, often equipped with doormen and all sorts of services, which represent quintessential New York old money. The area is also jam-packed with world-famous cultural, literary, and artistic landmarks. Joan Didion, Renata Adler, and Sylvia Plath all sojourned at the now defunct Barbizon Hotel for Women (only)—renamed "The Amazon" in Plath's *The Bell Jar*, at 140 East 63rd Street. *The Catcher in the Rye*'s Holden Caulfield's parents are also neighborhood residents.

The Upper East Side is home to Museum Mile along Fifth Avenue, on the east side of Central Park, with such prestigious institutions as the Metropolitan Museum of Art, the Jewish Museum, and the Solomon R. Guggenheim Museum, among a long list of other remarkable places. Possibly the best French bookshop in all of America, Albertine, is located on Museum Mile, too. The Carlyle, one avenue east of Museum Mile, was once home to Ludwig Bemelmans and is now home to the most beloved Bemelmans Bar. The neighborhood is peppered with architectural treasures—buildings and institutions that each carry a fascinating piece of history, whether literary or otherwise, we would all love to learn about.

The Frick Art Reference Library
10 East 71st Street

The Frick Collection currently stands on a piece of land—on Fifth Avenue between 70th and 71st streets—that once belonged to Robert Lenox, the father of James Lenox, who founded the Lenox Library, which also stood on that plot of land until its destruction in 1912. Henry Clay Frick acquired the land, destroyed the Lenox Library, and built his home, which is now the current Frick Collection.

If this were a museum or an arts guide to New York, the Frick Collection would obviously be one of the marquee attractions. Something not everybody knows, however, is that there is actually also a wonderful library within the premises. There are a few rules attached—it is only open to adults aged eighteen and older, and you must bring a form of identification and register for access. The library is widely regarded as a specialized research institution, more so than a library open to the general public. Unlike the museum itself, though, the library is free to visit. It boasts a particularly large and important collection of art and art-history research material.

Founded in 1920 by Helen Clay Frick (the daughter of Henry Clay Frick, who died one year earlier) as a memorial to her father, the library was housed in a few different locations throughout the Frick, before opening to the public in 1935 in the six-story building behind the museum, where it stands today. The library's collections focus on art of the Western tradition from the fourth century AD to the mid-twentieth century, and mainly include information about paintings, drawings, sculpture, prints, and illuminated manuscripts.

John Steinbeck's apartment
190 East 72nd Street

Along the winding booklover's path this guide has been following, it has sometimes proven difficult to authentically verify whether or not certain authors actually lived where rumors have suggested they have. The winner of the 1962 Nobel Prize for Literature John Steinbeck, though, most definitely lived at 190 East 72nd Street. At the time of writing, the apartment he lived in was on the market for close to five million dollars; the author's desk and study were included in the sale, and in some of the seller's materials on the place, there were comments from Steinbeck's granddaughter reminiscing about the apartment and the desk her grandfather "Fa" used to write on.

Steinbeck lived his last few years in the lavish Uptown apartment with his third wife, Elaine Anderson, until his passing in 1968. There is a whole room in the apartment dedicated to Steinbeck, where you will be able to see said desk, along with notes and posters, supposedly left intact, if you're able to purchase the property or become friends with the new owners. It is also known that the author wrote a lot in Sag Harbor.

Unlike Hemingway, California-native Steinbeck's relationship to New York seemed much less rocky and far more admiring. Though he does refer to the city, in a 1953 *New York Times* article, as being ugly, dirty, clogged with traffic, and competitive, he also famously stated that "once you have lived in New York and it has become your home, no place else is good enough."

Bemelmans Bar
35 East 76th Street

Named after the Scottish essayist Thomas Carlyle, the Carlyle Hotel was built by Moses Ginsberg, the grandfather of American novelist Rona Jaffe. Established in 1930, the combination luxury and residential hotel was nicknamed "the New York White House" during the John F. Kennedy administration. For the last ten years of his life, President Kennedy owned an apartment on the 34th floor, and guests such as Marilyn Monroe would sneak in for visits through secret tunnels.

Undoubtedly, the absolute best part of the famed and beautiful Carlyle is Bemelmans Bar. With its walls made up of murals painted by Ludwig Bemelmans (after whom the place was named), the Art Deco piano bar with its 24-karat gold-leaf-covered ceiling opened in 1947. Upmarket, exquisite, and atmospheric, the bar boasts the only surviving Bemelmans commission open to the public.

Bemelmans—the creator of Madeline, among many other genius characters, and often referred to as everybody's favorite storyteller and artist—reimagined animals in Central Park engaging in "adult activities," such as ice skating, picnicking, eating at a café, painting, holding an umbrella, or just strolling around. The artist painted the ravishing and playful murals in exchange for a year and a half's worth of lodgings at the Carlyle Hotel for him and his family.

The Legacy of Bemelmans Bar
Like the perfect cocktail, artist and author Ludwig Bemelmans' murals in Bemelmans Bar combine good taste and sophistication with a dash of wit. Bemelmans' depiction of New York's Central Park has been a beloved landmark for more than half a century. Commissioned in 1947 Ludwig Bemelmans, creator of the renowned *Madeline* Children's books, asked only for rooms at The Carlyle in exchange for his creation. Today, bar patrons enjoy a privileged view of the legendary murals, the artist's only surviving commission open to the public, in an atmosphere suffused with classic New York glamour.

On a Monday, before his legendary set at the Café Carlyle, you may be able to catch a glimpse of Woody Allen sitting in the far left corner of the room, mentally rehearsing for his clarinet performance, perhaps . . . Their cocktails are delicious, but very strong. Beware.

Gagosian Shop
976 Madison Avenue

Gagosian Gallery is not just one of the most prominent and well-respected contemporary art galleries in the world, it is also home to a wonderful decade-old bookshop. (There is one in Paris, too, but that is another story.) Filled not only with a remarkable collection of rare books, artists' books, and catalogues, the Upper East Side bookshop is made up of all sorts of desirable gadgets, special prints, posters, toys for kids, teacups for grannies or young tea lovers like myself, clocks for punctual people (unlike myself), Marc Newson knives for design fans, pillow covers for the cozy, jewelry for the fashionable, and intellectual home goods for any art, literature, or culture addict. In a spacious, airy, pleasant, and well-designed (by Selldorf Architects) setting, the Gagosian shop has a book or a gift for everybody.

The beautifully arranged display offers a great selection of new books of all genres, along with a vast array of very valuable and rare ones. Most of these are in stupendous condition and sometimes signed. In a way, parts of the shop double up as their own literary gallery.

Furthermore, Gagosian has been publishing its own quarterly magazine (interesting reads about the gallery's artists and art) since 2012, and it is of course a very strong name in the publishing of exhibition catalogues, which happen to be scholarly. The gallery also puts out catalogues raisonnés and artist monographs, most of which can be found at the New York bookstore. Go explore the rather enjoyable side of Madison Avenue and riffle through all these artistic treasures—you will be in for quite a treat.

Ursus Books & Gallery
50 East 78th Street

Once upon a time, the prestigious, rare book dealer Ursus (a name chosen by the owner's friend and artist Leonard Baskin, which means "bear" in Latin) graced the fancy corridors of the Carlyle. Opened in 1972 by Peter Kraus (the nephew of H. P. Kraus, described by William S. Reese as, "without a doubt, the most successful and dominant rare book dealer in the world in the second half of the twentieth century"), Ursus Books first started off as a dealer in scholarly art books and rare books of all kinds. It was soon followed by Ursus Prints, dealing in rare decorative prints, which was immediately incorporated within Ursus Books.

After a twenty-eight-year stint at the Carlyle, Kraus moved into 699 Madison, which was originally designed as a mini version of London's famous department store, Fortnum & Mason. These days, the specialized and sophisticated little shop is located in a much more discreet—and, to my taste, very refined—location in the back left corner on the first floor of a typical Upper East Side apartment building. The door might sometimes be closed, but there is a sign on it (like one of those hotel "do not disturb" signs) inviting you in. If you are unsure where to go and think you are in the wrong place, the helpful but quiet doorman will show you to it. The books in the shop are beautifully displayed and organized, and the people working there are friendly and knowledgeable.

Ursus is filled with all sorts of artistic treasures. It is said to stock the largest collection of catalogues raisonnés anywhere in the world. For nearly half a century now, Ursus has been renowned among artists and collectors for offering some of the best new and out-of-print books on any particular artist or subject (it was my dad, who is in his late sixties, who initially told me about Ursus, which he used to frequent during his early visits to the city). They tend to specialize in, though are not limited to, illustrated books of all periods, from the fifteenth through the twenty-first centuries.

If you happen to be looking for an exceptional copy of a rare art or illustrated book of any kind, Ursus should definitely be your first stop. The lovely little shop's stock is not gigantic, but they have lots more in storage in Harlem, so just ask if you're looking for something in particular and don't see it on the shop's meticulously curated shelves. In a profile of Kraus by Jill Adams of Eidolon House, he states that in this time of digital media, "books are more important now than ever. They are the physical manifestation of everything which makes up our civilization."

Albertine
972 Fifth Avenue

When I first heard about Albertine, it was like the second coming of the Marquis de Lafayette. I am French, and while croque-monsieurs, croissants, or special shampoo and laundry detergent are things I couldn't care less about bringing to America from home, there are few things I love more than French literature and the way Grasset or Flammarion books smell, feel, and, of course, read.

Most of what I read is in French. Weirdly enough, before Albertine, there weren't many places where you could find French books in New York. Then came Albertine, and not only were my problems solved, but a whole array of things ensued—from fun events to cool French-looking notebooks, and volumes and volumes of contemporary and classic titles from thirty French-speaking countries, all set in the most perfect and chic ode to French culture and literature.

The setting is so perfect and over-the-top impressive, that when you first enter the historic Payne Whitney mansion (fittingly designed by Stanford White, who is responsible for the Washington Square Arch), it almost seems absurd that it is home to a bookshop. But Albertine is not a simple bookshop; Albertine is the magical project imagined by the Cultural Services of the French Embassy. It embodies French cultural wealth and intellectual sophistication in a modern way and "brings to life the French government's commitment to French-American intellectual exchange."

For any French person living in New York, Albertine not only provides the most essential and desired books; it also nurtures a strong sense of community within its splendid two-floor space, thanks to its frequent and welcoming events, from lectures to classes and book signings. Another very respectable endeavor of Albertine's is its compliance with the French law: book prices cannot be reduced by more than 5 percent. This protects "a rich network of publishers and booksellers in France and nourishes its biblio-diversity." That is very French and I love it—I would rather pay a bit more if I am supporting the publishing industry and its authors.

To find out a little more about this French reader's paradise, I decided to ask Deputy Cultural Counselor Hervé Ferrage a few questions.

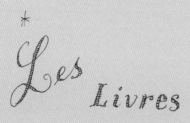

Albertine has approximately 14,000 books for sale. Are they all in French?

Albertine has a wide variety of classic and contemporary francophone literature in French and in English translation. Books in English make up approximately one quarter of our collection, which includes many genres: fiction, nonfiction, arts, cooking, young adult, graphic novels, poetry, and rare books, among others.

Describe Albertine in a few words.

Bookstores have always held an important place in the lives of French people, and we actually count over thirty-two thousand bookstores in France (versus twenty-one thousand in the United States), so Albertine brings to New York City this well-established tradition of independent French bookstores.

But Albertine is more than a bookstore; it is also a reading room where members of the community can come and immerse themselves in French literature for hours. Since Albertine opened in 2014, it has transformed into a cultural and intellectual hub that hosts hundreds of lively events on a weekly basis. These events involve prominent French and American artists, thinkers, and writers, including Alain Badiou, Leïla Slimani, Edouard Louis, Edwidge Danticat, Salman Rushdie, and Valeria Luiselli.

What was the original idea and inspiration behind Albertine? How did the project come about?

Albertine opened with the aim to provide a window into French culture in New York City and the United States. The second floor of Albertine, furnished with comfortable sofas, coffee tables, and wooden shelves, was designed to feel like an intimate library—much like a private library you would find in someone's home—and functions as a reading room as well as a bookshop. Since Albertine's opening, it has organized, with the Cultural Services, the Festival Albertine: an annual transdisciplinary series of discussions with French and American authors, artists, and thinkers on topics relevant to both countries. Under the curation of author and journalist Ta-Nehisi Coates (2016) and author and activist Gloria Steinem (2017), the past two editions have attracted several thousands of visitors apiece.

What sorts of events does Albertine put on in New York? Would you say they cater more to a French or a New York audience? What would you say is Albertine's role both in the New York bookselling industry and in the French expat community?

Since its inception, Albertine has hosted two or three events per week touching on various topics, from literature to politics, food, history, and the arts. These events—which are free and open to the public and are also available online via livestream—include book launches, as well as talks that pair together French thinkers with their American peers to encourage French-American intellectual exchange. These events draw both francophone New Yorkers and American Francophiles who are curious about French culture and looking to discover influential figures in contemporary French literature and art. The majority of our events are in English. For the past two years, Albertine has organized an annual reader's choice award, the Albertine Prize, honoring a French book in English translation. The Albertine Prize echoes a long tradition of initiatives developed by the literature department of the Cultural Services, such as French Voices, a program that aims to encourage the development of French literature in translation on the American market.

Aside from opening a place like Albertine, what else do you think can be done in New York to promote French culture or to support the publishing industry? What is the greatest enemy of the French publishing industry abroad?

An important challenge for us to take into account is that in the American book market, translation represents only 3 percent of all the books published in the United States. We've developed programs to promote French literature in translation here. One of our major initiatives is the aforementioned Albertine Prize, now in its second edition, which promotes contemporary French literature in translation. Antoine Volodine's *Bardo or Not Bardo* won the prize its first year, and Anne Garréta's *Not One Day* emerged triumphant in 2018. For us, this is a way to bring contemporary French literature to the local scene and to introduce our young authors to an American audience.

Additionally, in order to support the promotion of French titles in this country, the Cultural Services collaborates with American publishing houses to publish French books and promote French titles as soon as they find a publication house. Our French Voices Prize, currently in its eleventh year, embodies this mission.

On a rolling basis, the Cultural Services supports and contributes to book tours of French authors in the United States, such as those by Mathias Enard and Leïla Slimani over the past years, or Eric Vuillard (2017 winner of the Prix Goncourt), Léonora Miano and Gaël Faye (2016 winner of the Prix Goncourt des Lycéens), whom we are hosting for discussions at Albertine as part of their upcoming American tours.

What are the biggest challenges of running a foreign-language bookshop? Are most customers French?

There are many challenges in operating a foreign-language bookstore: keeping up with both the new French and American publications, staying on top of the book buzz in the two languages despite the distance (for the French titles), and hosting events that will resonate with both communities.

One of our challenges in attracting an American audience that is not familiar with translations is the misconception that one must speak French to attend our programs and events at Albertine, when these are actually targeted toward an English-speaking American audience.

Albertine's audience is composed of Francophones in New York, French expats, and American Francophiles. Located on New York City's Museum Mile and across the street from the Metropolitan Museum of Art, Albertine also benefits from a large number of tourists every year. Francophone communities come to Albertine in search of contemporary fiction, nonfiction, and children's books, whereas American readers are more drawn to classics. These are our most sought-after categories.

The New York Society Library
53 East 79th Street

The New York Society Library is officially the oldest library in the city open to the public. It was founded in 1754 by a civic-minded group of men who believed that "a well-stocked collection of books would help the city prosper." A wise statement, which led this group of six young professionals to set up shop in the old City Hall, before having a few stints in other parts of Downtown New York—at various locations in the FiDi, TriBeCa, and most notably at 109 University Place, a gorgeous building (sadly no longer there), which neighbor Willa Cather used very regularly.

The ravishing townhouse on one of the busier crosstown streets of the Upper East Side (79th Street) in which the NYSL operates today was acquired by the library in the mid-1930s. The two combined townhouses previously belonged to a family that had already done the conversion into one, and the result is majestic. Brilliantly organized in such a way that makes it seem highly efficient to work from, the Library houses many studious little areas to write, research, or read. The best one to me was almost like a charming hole with a table, chair, and lamp down a few steps off the art history room, which is also home to architecture, music, cartoons, gallery catalogues, and sports books, too. Calming, serene, and even more quiet than a church, the nook is also ornamented with two divine wood panels rescued from the former University Place location. Among many of the convenient and modernized rooms—most containing large, practical tables equipped with power sockets and lamps spread out spaciously—there are also tiny study rooms, almost like a miniature soundproof private cubicle or a recording booth that you can reserve all to yourself (at no cost). If you wish to peruse leisurely, there is also a gigantic room with extremely high ceilings, where computers are not permitted: you can read the papers or a recently borrowed novel in a comfy armchair by the chimney in what feels like a lavish centuries-old European hotel lobby.

In fact, the place generally feels like a superbly laid out deluxe hotel, in which there are not guest rooms but book rooms, filled with shelves and shelves of all types of literary treats. The collection prides itself in being not too scholarly nor academic, but also not too general—a perfect mix. Organized in an incredibly intelligent way, the two combined houses were redesigned to maintain the high-ceilinged rooms on one side of the building for studying, working, and browsing in a pleasant environment, while the other side of the building was divided up into rooms half the height in order to be able to store more of the books from their wonderfully rich collection.

The staff is beyond friendly, and if I wasn't such an avid fan and supporter of the NYPL system and a Downtown resident, I would splurge on the yearly membership fees in a heartbeat—these are surprisingly not high at all, given what the NYSL has to offer. A definite must for any bibliophile, even if it is just to sit and read the papers in the reference room (which is directly in front of you as you enter and also the only room open to nonmembers), or take a quick tour of the marvelous grounds.

New York Psychoanalytic Society & Institute
247 East 82nd Street

Established more than a century ago, the New York Psychoanalytic Society and Institute serves as the oldest psychoanalytic society in the United States. The Society was founded in 1911 by Abraham Arden Brill, a public advocate for psychoanalytic ideas, and, more importantly, the first translator of Freud's writings into English. Modelled on the Berlin Psychoanalytic Institute, the New York Psychoanalytic Institute was established by the Society in 1931.

The Abraham A. Brill Library is in the NYPSI building on a quiet street of the Upper East Side, and is the world's largest psychoanalytic library. With forty thousand volumes spanning the literature of psychoanalysis from its founding to today, it represents a unique resource to the psychoanalytic community. Members and candidates of the NYPSI, as well as psychoanalytic and scholarly communities, can use the library freely, which is open most afternoons until 9 p.m. The general public is able to use the library for research purposes only.

Thomas J. Watson Library & Nolen Library at The Metropolitan Museum of Art
1000 Fifth Avenue

Did you know that when you are nervously tiptoeing around the glorious and jaw-dropping Metropolitan Museum, you are also stepping over some 650,000 books hidden below ground?

Not everybody is aware of this, but the Metropolitan Museum of Art is not just two million square feet of unbelievable sculptures, paintings, and all sorts of artwork from the past five thousand years. The legendary and iconic museum also holds a few of its own in-house libraries. The Thomas J. Watson Library and the Nolen Library—rather different from each other—are the main ones, both located within the premises.

Walk to the main staircase just past the Great Hall, bear an immediate left on the first floor, and there you will find the Thomas J. Watson Library. Known as a research center with one of the most comprehensive collections in the world, the books, periodicals, ephemera, and various forms of resources the Watson Library has available mostly relate to the history of art. The whole collection comprises nearly a million volumes, 650,000 of which are kept underground below the museum, while most of the rest are in storage upstate with a variety of other academic and unrelated material. No appointment is necessary to consult at the Watson Library, but you will need to register, and might have to check some of your belongings into a locker.

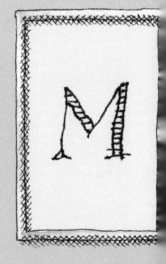

In the Uris Center for Education, located on the ground floor closer to the 81st Street entrance of the museum, you will come across the Nolen Library. Slightly more accessible to the general public of all ages, the Nolen holds all kinds of material on its open shelves, ranging from exhibition catalogues to graphic novels and a large selection of children's books. Though the entirety of the Nolen's collection is not as great as that of the Watson (a little more than ten thousand items), this concise library provides a wonderful space for people of all (art-related) interests and generations. Programs, story time hours, and curriculum resources are aplenty in this user-friendly hideout. Teachers are also welcome to bring their classes with them, so long as they arrange for it in advance.

There are also other libraries in the Met, such as the Onassis Library for Hellenic and Roman Art, a small Greek and Roman Art library, which is only open to researchers or students and museum staff. The Leonard A. Lauder Research Center for Modern Art is another place where someone specializing in the study of modern art could find lots of information and resources. Then there is the Costume Institute's Irene Lewisohn Costume Reference Library for anything fashion-related, as well as the Antonio Ratti Textile Center and Reference Library, which, if I were a designer or a fashion student, I would probably have an urgent desire to visit. For arts of the Italian Renaissance, try the Robert Lehman Collection Library, if you happen to be a qualified researcher. As an extra piece of information, there is a photo library called the Joyce F. Menschel Photography Library, which also has restricted access.

Last but not least is the Robert Goldwater Library. It is home to all the contents of the now defunct Library of the Museum of Primitive Art, which used to be on West 54th Street before closing in 1975. The Robert Goldwater Library opened to the public in 1982, and was named for the first director of the Museum of Primitive Art, a renowned scholar. The collection is now part of the Met's Department of the Arts of Africa, Oceania, and the Americas.

Farther uptown, the beautiful Met Cloisters has its own library and archive center—The Cloisters Library and Archives—also open to researchers and by appointment only. While the newly installed contemporary wing of the Met, the Met Breuer, has no library as of yet, the Whitney Museum—which was previously on the premises—used to be the next-door neighbor to one of the most notoriously respected bookshops, Books and Company, which was in operation from 1978 to 1997 and owned by Jeannette Watson, who is now an author.

Logos Bookstore
1575 York Avenue

Logos Bookstore on the far eastern Upper East Side carries a large selection of Judeo-Christian books, as well as Bibles. Harris Healy is the owner of this bookshop, which is part of the Logos Bookstore Association, a national franchise headquartered in Kent, Ohio. Said to have the largest religious selection in Manhattan, the shop also stocks children's books if you want to give your kids a religious education, or in case they are just curious.

The delightful-looking little shop—painted with a green storefront—sells greeting cards and gift items too. Logos also hosts events such as book signings, children's story times, and reading groups. If you are not in the mood to be social like that, just grab whatever you feel like studying up on and head to the lovely Carl Schurz park, which is only one block away.

The Writing Room
1703 Second Avenue

Someone I have in my day-to-day life and truly appreciate is Miguel. Part extraordinary actor, part wonderful doorman in our building, he is one of the nicest people I have met in recent years and tells the best stories ever. I have the pleasure of seeing him on Friday and Saturday mornings, and on some random evenings, depending on how late I go out. I do sometimes wish I saw him more, though, as he is truly a magical soul.

Long before he worked in our vicinity, Miguel had a job at the legendary Uptown celebrity haunt Elaine's. As the youngest apprentice, Elaine completely took him under her wing. Apparently not a fan of youngsters (other employees' ages ranged between seventy-six and somewhere in their fifties), Miguel was an exception to her strict rules. She loved him, and really trained him during those formative years. Miguel loved it there, too, and, as a great storyteller, told me all about how crazy it was, how rowdy it would get, how special and privileged it felt to work in the company of such brilliant authors.

Miguel said that one day, as the bon vivant that he is, he decided to pay a visit to the Writing Room, the restaurant that opened in Elaine's location. It now serves the neighborhood with modern American cuisine and a bookish décor, which obviously pays tribute to the locale's previous tenant. Miguel was very well received, shown all around the place, and almost treated like royalty. The name itself pays homage to its legendary predecessor, as does the whole ambiance: photos of authors and celebrities, from Gay Talese to Jackie Onassis, adorn the walls, as do shelves filled with handpicked books of all kinds. Even the outside façade was restored to look like Elaine's used to. The food may not be as engaging as the stories told within, but perhaps one should pay a visit for the atmosphere and the anecdotes alone.

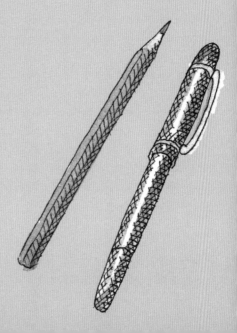

Carnegie Hill Books
206 East 90th Street by appointment only
Tel: 212-410-9085

Carnegie Hill Books falls right into a category of bookshops that I deem very much appreciated. It defines itself as a rare-book provider, specializing in architecture, modern design, interior design, furniture, gardens, fashion, photography, illustration, and, most importantly New York City. Ann Brockschmidt (who ran the out-of-print and rare-book department at Archivia, the Decorative Arts Bookshop, for more than twelve years until it closed in 2003) and Doug Mills operate Carnegie Hill Books from their home and will host you there by appointment. Though their book selection does indeed qualify as "rare, collectible, and hard-to-find," the prices are far more advantageous and accessible than some of those shops in the rare and antiquarian section of this book. Ann and Doug have extensive knowledge in their areas of expertise and offer optimal customer service— worth scheduling a visit if you are on the hunt for something special in the topics they have to offer.

92nd Street Y
1395 Lexington Avenue

Founded almost one and a half centuries ago, the 92nd Street Young Men's and Young Women's Hebrew Association was originally opened as a Jewish community and cultural center. It is mostly known for bringing people together, and hosting an excellent series of author events in the fields of literature, art, and education. Today, the 92nd Street Y is a multifaceted cultural institution, which serves people of all races and faiths. As one of the city's most prestigious venues, it offers countless activities in all fields of the arts, and specifically within literary ones. It was in 1935 that William Kolodney became Educational Director at 92Y. He fostered a wide variety of educational programs, including the creation of the poetry center—now known as the Unterberg Poetry Center —which has often been led by prominent writers, such as the award-winning poet Karl Kirchwey.

Hosting all sorts of series of talks and conversations between notable authors, as well as literary readings, the 92nd Street Y is a world-renowned place for social, poetic, literary, and cultural events.

La Librairie des Enfants
163 East 92nd Street

Cross over 92nd Street and walk half a minute to La Librairie des Enfants—an adorable shop all the way up in one of the quieter parts of the Upper East Side. It sits one block over from a beautiful old wooden house, which is now a landmark. La Librairie des Enfants's façade and storefront is just as cute. Painted in an old-fashioned bright red, the shop from the outside resembles something between a fire station and a quaint Parisian café; it seems like you are stepping out of time when you walk in.

Quintessentially French, there is a tiny borrowing library occupying the back couple of shelves to the right. The heartbreakingly low table in front of the shelves filled with books (organized by age groups) makes you just imagine all the small French boys and girls who come over for reading hour, French class, or any sorts of activities the owner Lynda Ouhenia-Hudson and her colleagues host on a weekly basis.

You can also join games, dancing, or cooking classes, which makes the shop feel a bit like a community-driven place. There are also marionette shows, which put a smile on my face and reminded me of my childhood—they were not my favorite, but growing up in France meant you often went (and were obliged to participate). A definite must if you are French or just a Francophile. Also a good place to stop and buy a kid's book—they have translated English ones too, if you can't speak French!

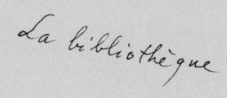

The Corner Bookstore
1313 Madison Avenue

A Carnegie Hill staple since 1978, the Corner Bookstore prides itself in carrying "only the best of the best" in all sections of the store, including history, biography, travel, cookbooks, parenting, poetry, mysteries, and art. The Corner Bookstore, which is now forty years old, is an utterly perfect local bookshop. Its size is just right—it was a pharmacy for fifty years before becoming the bookshop it is now—and the space is full of beautiful and original details from the 1920s, from tinned ceilings and wood cabinetry to a terrazzo floor, all of which were covered with grime and paint before being restored by Ray, one of the owners.

That same Ray decided on the name "The Corner Bookstore" because, as it was on the corner of Madison and 93rd Street, he believed it would inevitably end up being known as that anyway. He affixed that very appropriate name on the storefront with wooden letters cut out with a jigsaw and gilded with 14-karat gold-leaf foil. I must say, it does look very nice with the red, as does the entire inside of the shop. What I loved the most was the old-fashioned cash register.

Something else I liked about the Corner Bookstore was its very authentic way of operating in the manner a local bookshop would. It has a bit of everything, all displayed beautifully and in a very serene and peaceful, bookish atmosphere. The staff is friendly, and, unsurprisingly, I read that they throw an "Open House Christmas Eve Party" every year with free Champagne and homemade cookies for the neighborhood—something all local businesses should consider doing, but seldom do! (Santa is in attendance at the shindig too.)

Kitchen Arts & Letters
1435 Lexington Avenue

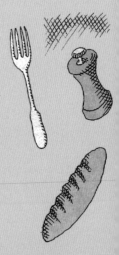

Ever so slightly different from Bonnie Slotnick's and Joanne Hendricks's cookbook shops, Kitchen Arts & Letters is your Uptown bookshop offering anything food- or drink-related. With a huge inventory offering much more than just cookbooks, Kitchen Arts & Letters also carries titles on food history and scholarship, and an extensive selection of technical manuals. All in all they offer an excellent collection of great food writing. You can easily get a sense of that when you pay them a visit. A must if you intend on cooking up a feast, or even if you just want to read about one!

Shakespeare & Co.
939 Lexington Avenue
2020 Broadway

I was at first a tad reticent to give my full attention to New York's Shakespeare & Co. bookshops, based simply on the fact that I am French, and that they are not affiliated in the slightest with the legendary Parisian Shakespeare and Company, whose shops have been a fixture of the Left Bank for a century. The latter, of course, holds a very sweet spot in my heart, as it probably does for most French people. But this is a rare instance of two entities sharing not only a name but a parallel level of importance; New York's Shakespeare & Co. being one of the more respected and long-standing icons of bookselling in the city.

I remember rather clearly stumbling into Lexington Avenue's Shakespeare & Co. for the first time some fifteen years ago or so, when I was still a student and not yet a New York resident. A young and adventurous visitor at the time, I was looking for a toilet, a book, a cup of tea, something warm and pleasant, a place to take a break in the middle of what can sometimes be quite an active hustle and bustle of the Upper East Side. The store felt studenty and friendly, with books of high quality and intellectual pedigree.

The shop still stands and nowadays is known as the official brick-and-mortar bookstore for Hunter College—which confirmed that studenty feel to it on my first visit! Shakespeare & Co. has another branch on the Upper West Side, and they are in fact expanding. They have a location in Philadelphia (as they fully intend to go national), as well as plans for a Downtown location to open in Greenwich Village. Despite this expansion, Shakespeare & Co. still sees itself as independent, in the sense that its CEO Dane Neller—also CEO and founder of On Demand Books, the company responsible for the renowned and beloved Espresso Book Machine—wants the shops to be small and localized. Neller would like Shakespeare & Co. to become "the biggest little book-shop in the world"—and if the atmosphere and selection of this original and iconic branch are anything to go by, it just might.

Tom Freston

Legendary founding member of MTV, worldwide traveler, and current inhabitant of Andy Warhol's old townhouse

Tom Freston

You've spent much of your life traveling (including your early years residing in Kabul and New Delhi as a textile exporter). How does your book collection reflect your travels?

Books about Asia and everywhere else I've been; fiction, nonfiction and, especially, photography collections are the backbone of my book collection. In addition, I have shelves of old travel guides, going back to the 1950s. I even have the original *Lonely Planet* by Tony Wheeler, published in 1973, as well as guide books on Afghanistan and Kabul from the 1970s when tourists went there.

You're a founder of MTV. What's one of the greatest music books ever written? What's the music bible?

There are so many in the music category. Some I loved would be Timothy White's *Catch a Fire: The Life of Bob Marley*. That's a real classic and has had many printings. I knew Tim and unfortunately he passed away with a heart attack at a very early age. *Please Kill Me* by Legs McNeil, on the history of punk rock, is truly entertaining. But king is Peter Guralnick's *Last Train to Memphis* about the rise of Elvis Presley, himself the king.

You live in Andy Warhol's old house—how come?

I bought Andy Warhol's old townhouse in 2000. I had been living in TriBeCa for nearly twenty years and my wife wanted to move uptown. The house had been empty for thirteen years before I bought it, since 1987 when Andy died. Safe to say, it needed a lot of work. I used to have a show on MTV with Andy Warhol, in the early days, called *Andy Warhol's Fifteen Minutes*. He would have me over for lunch once or twice a year at The Factory, so I did have a small amount of personal history with him. The lunches were always interesting and I often left with a signed lithograph. Anyhow, it was a beautiful house, the price was right, and it sounded like the perfect thing for me to move in. It definitely had a cool vibe. I'm still here.

In your opinion, what is the best place to acquire a book in New York?

It's hard to beat the Strand down on lower Broadway. I also like Argosy Book Store on East 59th Street. It has a pretty good collection of old and rare books. For travel books there is Idlewild Books on lower Seventh Avenue. It's named after the original name for the John F. Kennedy airport, a place where a lot of trips begin.

***How have the music scene and the literary scene changed since MTV was
first born?***

The music and literary scenes in New York have changed quite a bit in the last
thirty-five years. Everything is a little more corporate and a little less independent.
And there are a lot fewer choices. So many good venues have disappeared, casu-
alties of high rents and so on—great places like The Bottom Line. Chains have
moved in, places like the Hard Rock Cafe where they staple guitars to the wall.
There seems to be a bit of a reversal of that these days. I hope it continues. The
idea that there might be a cool little jazz bar down the street on the corner is sort
of a lost notion, though, even in Greenwich Village nowadays.

***What's the most precious (in rarity, or monetary or sentimental value)
book that you've ever acquired? Please tell me about it.***

Two of my first-edition books have special meaning to me. One is Jack Kerouac's
The Dharma Bums. Kerouac has a very big influence on me. When I got out of
college, I read it in paperback and was inspired to go hiking in the High Sierra
Mountains of California, like the protagonist, searching for satori up there at high
altitude. One day, walking up Madison Avenue, I saw it in a bookshop window
and ran right in and got it. It opens up with a great passage about him jumping
on a train in Los Angeles heading north and then jumping off in Carpenteria and
sleeping on the beach there. I'd forgotten about the opening. A great piece of
synchronicity is I now have a house right near the Carpenteria beach. I keep that
book out there.

The other book is *Golden Earth*, a beautifully written, dreamy travelogue by Norman
Lewis about his travels in the golden land of Burma in the mid 1950s. It was a very
special and peaceful time there before the Ne Win dictatorship came down like a
black cloud and lasted fifty years. I have traveled a lot in that country in the last
twenty years and would have so loved to have been able to be there then. I snapped
it up at a street stall on Portobello Road in London one morning years ago.

As a frequent traveler, what book are you bringing on your next trip?

I always bring books about the country I'm visiting, fiction or otherwise. I also,
if possible—and it sounds kind of corny—bring along a copy of the *Lonely Planet*
guide for that country. That's a bit of a tradition for me. I find they consolidate a
lot of history, along with the usual travel information, into a nice compact format.
I may be one of their best customers and have piles of them. I have four just on
Morocco that span several different decades. It's kind of fun to go back and read
the old ones. Prices sure have gone up.

Nan & Gay Talese

This legendary New York couple needs no introduction, but if I had to . . . Nan is an American editor and veteran of the New York publishing industry. Gay is a best-selling author of fourteen books, a reporter for the *New York Times*, the *New Yorker,* and *Esquire*, always impeccably dressed in a dashing suit. Both work and have an exceedingly high amount of books under the roof of their Upper East Side townhouse.

This interview took place in the form of a succession of multiple correspondences via email. Here are some extracts of said correspondence:

Dear Cleo,

I can tell you a little bit about our house and its books:

On the first floor are leather-bound and foreign editions of Gay's books. Also books by friends.

On the second floor in the rear of the house are biographies; at the front are the books published under my imprint: Nan A. Talese / Doubleday.

On the third floor is fiction (in the rear of the house). In the front of the house are some other books that I have published at Random House, Simon & Schuster, and Houghton Mifflin.

There is another collection: Modern Library, etc., mostly classics, in the "bunker," where Gay writes.

The fourth floor is Gay's, where he keeps his clothes, more books, particularly ones he used for research.

It is true the Upper East Side used to be famous for writers, but I now *think the location is Brooklyn.*

For some reason my computer is only typing in italics... Sorry about the delay but the photographer took all day.

Best,
Nan

What do you love the most about your respective jobs as writer and editor? What are the most challenging or difficult parts of those jobs? Are any of those traits unique to being in New York?

It is a difficult job to write, but Gay has been successful and he does like the research. I love my work, which mostly involves reading—and then the hard part is guessing what the book will sell and making an offer to publish.

How does the city of New York and its inhabitants inspire your writing and the characters in some of your work? Do you both like working under the same roof? Does it work well, or do you ever step on each other's toes?

New York doesn't inspire me especially and we both like working in the house. Gay has his "bunker," which is a beautiful space where he can be private (no noise, telephone, or knocking on the door). I work on the second floor.

Gay & Nan Talese

Antiquarian & Rare Booksellers

There are books for "normal" people—the average reader who is interested in more or less everything qualifies as the "normal" I am referring to here. Then there are books for the others: the 1 percent. The people who know exactly what they want or need and, more importantly, the people who have the means to supply themselves with precisely that.

The following bookshops are not always visible or accessible to the "normal" people I was referring to. A lot of them are not directly on the street (they are sometimes on an upper-floor gallery), and most of them are only open by appointment. What they sell is usually very specialized and completely unaffordable, often only suitable for a collector or an expert in rare or antiquarian books, or someone who specializes in a particular field of academia. But if you happen to be looking for something very specific and quite expensive—or if you just fancy a little luxurious and extravagant browse—I thought it best to provide you with a list of some of the options available in Manhattan (starting downtown, and going upward).

The Antiquarian Booksellers' Association of America (ABAA) and the International League of Antiquarian Booksellers (ILAB) provide extensive knowledge on this subject matter and would also be of tremendous help in finding any great treasures in New York.

Below Midtown
New York Bound Books *2 Fifth Avenue, Suite 12F*
By mail and online. Manuscripts, prints, and drawings, with local history, atlases, and maps.

Govi Rare Books, c/o Ferrante Law Firm *5 West 19th Street, 10th Floor*
By appointment only. Bindings, books about books, early printings, manuscripts, old and rare books, specializing in humanism.

B&B Rare Books *30 East 20th Street, Suite 305*
Buy and sell nineteenth- and twentieth-century English and American literature, modern first editions, poetry, children's literature, signed books, as well as appraisal, binding, and repair.

Pryor-Johnson Rare Books *1123 Broadway, Suite 517*
Best to call before, though mostly open all day. Unusual, rare, and interesting books from the fifteenth century through to very recent editions. Particular strengths include signed modern first editions, photography, books about books, fine press, and Beat literature.

Michael R. Weintraub, Inc. *231 West 29th Street, Suite 1401*
By appointment only. Modern illustrated books, architecture, photography, decorative arts, and performing arts.

Midtown

Lion Heart Autographs *216 East 45th Street, Suite 1100*
By appointment only. Reference library of biographies, monographs, and specialized encyclopedias.

Justin G. Schiller, Ltd. *230 Park Avenue, 10th Floor*
Rare and collectible children's books in all languages and covering all time periods.

Bauman Rare Books *535 Madison Avenue*
A rarity in this specialized rare and antiquarian field, Bauman finds itself directly on the street, and in fact right in the middle of one of the busiest parts of Madison Avenue. It's difficult to miss this serene and beautiful—albeit a little stuffy—gallery amid the hustle and bustle of Midtown, with its neat and tidy shelves of leather-bound books and cabinets filled with expensive first editions and letters. Best known for their expertise and their exceptional variety of high-quality books, Bauman also has a gallery in Las Vegas and offices in Philadelphia.

Martayan Lan *70 East 55th Street, 6th Floor*
One of the leading dealers in rare books and manuscripts worldwide, covering the early fifteenth century all the way to 1800. Rare, illustrated, historically important books in fine condition, as well as antique maps.

J.N. Bartfield Galleries *60 West 55th Street, 5th Floor*
American, Western, and sporting art gallery, specializing in rare books, first editions, exhibition bindings, color plate books, Americana, press books, literature, and leather-bound sets and singles.

The Manhattan Rare Book Company *1050 Second Avenue, Gallery 90*
By appointment only. Outstanding books in fine condition, signed and unsigned, on all topics ranging from art to photography, history, religion, fashion, and many more.

East of the Park

James Cummins Bookseller *699 Madison Avenue, #7*
Quiet and pleasantly furnished oasis for booklovers with a carefully chosen, expertly catalogued, and broad-based selection of fine and rare books, manuscripts, and works of art; specializing in Bibles, sporting books, color plate books, private press, first editions, fine bindings, sets, English and American literature, as well as illustration art.

Daniel Crouch Rare Books NY *24 East 64th Street*
Antique atlases, maps, plans, sea charts, and voyages dating from the fifteenth to the nineteenth centuries, as well as fine prints, globes, and a selection of cartographic reference books.

PRPH Rare Books *26 East 64th Street, 3rd Floor*
Umberto Pregliasco's and Filippo Rotundo's new rare books and art gallery, offering manuscripts, early printings and incunabula, modern first editions, and illustrated books.

Imperial Fine Books *790 Madison Avenue, 6th Floor*
Leading specialist in leather-bound sets and fine bindings in all fields: literature, history, children's, sporting, color plate, illustrated, first editions, Cosway, jeweled, and exhibition bindings. Brightly lit, hospitable—and refreshingly affordable.

Sanctuary Books *790 Madison Avenue, Suite 604*
By appointment only. Varied inventory from all periods of printing, with a strong selection of original manuscript material and unique book creations that date from before Gutenberg up until, and including, contemporary artists' books.

Paulette Rose, Fine & Rare Books *10 East 70th Street*
By appointment only. By and about women, feminism, women writers, American, French, and British literature, dating from the sixteenth through to the twentieth century.

Richard C. Ramer, Old & Rare Books *225 East 70th Street, Suite 12F*
By appointment only. Rare books and manuscripts on Spain, Portugal, and their former overseas possessions in Latin America, Brazil, Africa, and Asia. Books recently published in Portugal, too.

Donald A. Heald, *124 East 74th Street*
By appointment only. Antiquarian books and prints in the areas of botany, ornithology, natural history, Americana, and Canadiana.

Marilyn Braiterman Antiquarian Bookseller *970 Park Avenue, Apt. 3S*
By appointment only. Decorative arts and design, architecture and landscape, press books and fine printings, sixteenth- to twentieth-century illustrated books, and Judaica.

Zucker Art Books *145 East 84th Street, Suite PHC*
By appointment only. Rare and antiquarian books and illustrated books by artists such as Picasso, Matisse, Miró, Chagall, Braque, Rouault, Léger, and others. Contemporary book publishing commissioned by artists and exhibitions.

Abby Schoolman Books *332 East 84th Street*
By appointment only. Specializes in contemporary art bookbinding and artists' books.

Musinsky Rare Books *176 West 87th Street*
By appointment only. Quirky and beautiful printed books, manuscripts, and prints from the incunable period to the mid-nineteenth century, mainly from Continental Europe and focusing on the humanities.

✳ Crawford Doyle Booksellers *21 East 90th Street*
By appointment only. Modern American and British fiction, from the twentieth and twenty-first centuries, as well as other titles of unusual interest, in art, biography, history, and science.

Rare Book Buyer (Adam Weinberger), *1510 Lexington Avenue, Apt. 9D*

Adam Weinberger has been involved in the rare books and manuscripts business for more than thirty years. Offering fair prices as well as free evaluations for rare books, Rare Book Buyer buys old and rare books, libraries, and estates nationwide.

West of the Park

Jonathan A. Hill *325 West End Avenue*

By appointment only. Specializing in science, medicine, natural history, bibliography, the history of book collecting, and early printed books.

Wurlitzer-Bruck *60 Riverside Drive*

By appointment only. Music antiquarian books.

David Bergman *211 West 85th Street, #BE*

By appointment only. Paleontology, natural history, evolution, graphic and decorative arts, and general stock.

E.K. Schreiber *285 Central Park West*

By appointment only. Specializes in pre-1700 Continental books, such as early printed books, incunabula, Renaissance humanism, early and important editions of the Greek and Latin classics, early illustrated books, emblem books, theology, and early Bibles (in Greek and Latin).

Pomander Books *211 West 92nd Street, Box 30*

By appointment only. Hard-to-find modern poetry—from T. S. Eliot to the Beats and the Language Poets; twentieth-century prose; first editions, signed books, association copies; and out-of-print books and "things" by Edward Gorey.

Gosen Rare Books & Old Paper *230 Riverside Drive*

By appointment only. Special antiquarian books, manuscripts, music, prints, autographed material, printed ephemera, and other selected material on paper.

Better Book Getter *310 Riverside Drive*

By appointment only. Rare and out-of-print books bought and sold, professional book search, library fulfillment, and acquisitions.

THE UPPER WEST SIDE

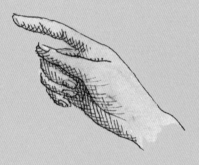

T

he Upper West Side is known as one of the nation's epicenters for cultural and political liberalism. Home to many artists, authors, and great savants, the neighborhood is historically depicted as a bastion of hope for an intellectual community of left-wing writers and thinkers.

The Upper West Side is dotted with places like the old Ansonia Hotel (now converted into apartments), of which Saul Bellow sings the praises in his fourth novel *Seize the Day*. It is also mined with cultural institutions and landmarks, such as the American Museum of Natural History or its neighboring New-York Historical Society, or even the statue of Dante, all sitting along the west side of Central Park. The Upper West Side is also where you picture most of Woody Allen's manic and brainy characters caught up in long dialogues, or strolling around looking for inspiration—or perhaps just searching for new books.

Dante Square
Intersection of Broadway, Columbus Avenue, and West 63rd Street

Geographically, within the New York City Department of Parks and Recreation, there seems to be some confusion around the exactitude of what is defined as Dante Park. But to avoid sending you around all the houses, it is roughly located at the intersection of Broadway, Columbus Avenue, and West 63rd Street—quite straightforward to me.

Famous for his *Divine Comedy*, which we all studied in school, I assume, Durante degli Alighieri, more commonly known as Dante (1295–1321), was a famous Florentine poet from the late middle ages. His *Divine Comedy* is considered to be the greatest Italian literary work, and the first one known to be written in Tuscan, instead of Latin.

There are Dante Squares (or Piazze) in most major Italian cities. The one I am most familiar with is the beautiful one in Naples. This American version of a piazza here in New York is right in front of Lincoln Center, and is graced with an Ettore Ximenes statue from 1921 of the famed poet (a twin statue can also be found at Meridian Hill Park in Washington, DC). It was Carlo Barsotti's idea (of the Italian-language American daily newspaper *Il Progresso Italo-Americano*) to have such a statue in New York. Now you can stop by and sit down on one of the benches near it, leaf through a copy of the *Divine Comedy*, and think of Dante's life, some 700 years ago in Italy.

Alice's Tea Cup
Chapter I: 102 West 73rd Street
Chapter II: 156 East 64th Street

Self-proclaimed most whimsical teahouse in New York, Alice's Tea Cup might actually be just that. To me, the idea of going for tea in an *Alice's Adventures in Wonderland*–themed café is almost Japanese. That said, anything with a theme (themed décor, themed menu, and themed everything) immediately seems Japanese, regardless of what it really is.

Alice's Tea Cup, however, is intrinsically a New York destination. Whether you choose to visit the Upper West Side (Chapter I) or the Upper East Side (Chapter II) location, you will not be disappointed. (There is also a Chapter III opening in Brooklyn in the near future.) Whichever charmingly painted café Alice fans choose, they will be literarily thrilled: the furniture matches the painted walls and the Alice theme, as does the menu (why not have "The Mad Morning" to start your day off like a Mad Hatter?), and the general vibe and ambiance are also quite Alice-like. It's a good place to go with a child before a walk through the park—but if you don't have one of your own, I suppose it is also okay to go with adults only to try the Tweedledees and Tweedledums.

Dante Alighieri

New-York Historical Society
170 Central Park West

Established in 1804 as the very first museum in New York, the New-York Historical Society is not just any kind of museum. It is a breathtaking and majestic institutional landmark that is completely impossible to miss, whether you are passing through New York on a visit or have been a long-time resident. For many reasons, the New-York Historical Society is also an essential literary epicenter.

One of the N-YHS's many attributes is its ability to curate a spectacular roster of remarkable literary heroes as some of its exhibition subjects. In the past few decades alone, some of the exhibitions the N-YHS has hosted have featured illustrations and objects from literary masterpieces. Some of these have included J. K.Rowling's *Harry Potter*; *Chitty Chitty Bang Bang! The Magical Car* showcasing Barney Tobey's illustrations; my all-time favorites, *Eloise* and *Madeline* exhibitions; and a "Superheroes in Gotham" exhibition. The Society also acts as guardian of the city's own history as a topic in general.

Another one of the N-YHS's exceedingly literary areas, which is impossible to ignore and more than a vital stop on this booklover's tour, is its very prestigious library. Unlike its museum, the library is free to use. Upon reaching out to the N-YHS, inquiring about the library and requesting a detailed description of it, I received the following text from the library staff:

"One of only 20 U.S. members of the prestigious Independent Research Libraries Association, the New-York Historical Society Library is widely recognized as a principal source of primary and secondary materials for the study of New York history, and one of the foremost American history research institutions in the world, ranking in pre-twentieth-century Americana with the New York Public Library and the Library of Congress. Because the New-York Historical Society has been collecting since the early decades of this country's founding, the Library collections are rich, deep, and diverse and include approximately 20,000 linear feet of manuscripts and archives—representing a nearly 50 percent increase as a result of the significant donation of the Time, Inc. Archive in November 2015; 350,000 books and pamphlets; 500,000 photographic prints and negatives;

560,000 drawings, plans, and blueprints in the architecture collections; 15,000 maps and atlases; 10,000 newspaper titles (including the fourth-largest collection of pre-1820 American newspaper titles in the United States); 275,000 prints and graphic artworks; 20,000 broadsides; 10,000 dining menus; the Bella C. Landauer Collection of Business and Advertising Ephemera, as well as smaller ephemeral collections that document New York City hotels, apartments, and office buildings; the events surrounding September 11, 2001; and Occupy Wall Street. Among the vast and varied manuscript and archival holdings are papers from the Colonial, Revolutionary War, Early Republic, and Civil War periods including: account books, diaries, journals, and other documents relating to the history of New York and the United States. The Library's 10,000 reels of microfilm, available by interlibrary loan, cover portions of all of its collections; the Library also subscribes to approximately 100 periodicals."

Additionally, the New-York Historical Society gives out book prizes. There are three of them: the Barbara and David Zalaznick Book Prize in American History, the New-York Historical Society Children's History Book Prize, and the Gilder Lehrman Prize for Military History.

The New-York Historical Society is an impressive place to visit. It should certainly not be missed! It sometimes has additional outposts, too, such as their summer teen-curated satellite Governors Island location. Its eleven founders declared that "without the aid of original record and authentic documents, history will be nothing more than a well-combined series of ingenious conjectures and amusing fables."

The Library of the American Museum of Natural History

Central Park West at 79th Street

Like so many of the other New York institutions, the breathtaking and fascinating American Museum of Natural History (filled with dinosaurs, animals, and nature of all kinds—just as fun for adults as for children of all ages) also has its very own library, which happens to be one of the largest natural history libraries in the world.

Established in 1869, when the museum first made its grand appearance west of Central Park, the AMNH Library mainly caters to the Museum's scientific staff. Its collection dates back to the fifteenth century, with a lot of the materials near impossible to find elsewhere.

Because the AMNH Library's collection is so extensive, some of the other New York–based libraries, such as the NYPL and the Columbia and NYU libraries, have sometimes chosen to make their natural history collections less thorough than some of their other ones. One of the most recent acquisitions of the AMNH Library is the 1997 incorporation of the Richard S. Perkin Collection in Astronomy and Astrophysics of the former Hayden Planetarium, with archives dating back to 1934 (one year before its opening). The fact that all these invaluable collections are combined under one roof and as a unique collection makes the AMNH Library vital to researchers, scholars, and anyone with any interest in the fields of natural history.

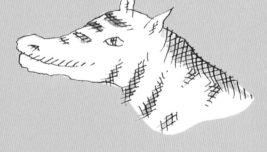

Book Culture

450 Columbus Avenue

536 West 112th Street

2915 Broadway

26-09 Jackson Avenue, Long Island City

Book Culture operates as an independent bookstore, with three branches on the Upper West Side, and a fourth one in Long Island City. The owner and original founder, Chris Doeblin, began with the creation of Labyrinth Books in 1997. Doeblin first started selling books in the 1980s at Papyrus bookstore at 114th and Broadway (later the location of his second Book Culture store). Doeblin had a vision to open an academic bookstore to serve the Upper West Side community he knew so well; so, with the help of Columbia University's Provost at the time, he opened his first store on 112th Street in a Columbia-owned space originally built for the Post Office.

In 2009, still with the support of Columbia and, of course, the Morningside Heights community, Book Culture opened on Broadway, continuing the tradition of there being an independent bookstore on the corner of 114th Street for the previous half century. Book Culture on Broadway prides itself on being a real community bookstore: "We are a meeting place, a fun place to stop and, above all, a real bookstore."

In 2014, Book Culture on Columbus opened in what used to be known as Endicott Booksellers, bringing Rick MacArthur (*Harper's Magazine* president and publisher) in as a third owner, along with Doeblin and Annie Hendrick. There is currently also a fourth location in Queens, on Jackson Avenue.

Book Culture is not an ordinary local bookshop. Book Culture is an Upper West Side movement to bring diversity in the representation of books and ideas, especially in the fields of "scholarly books, academic disciplines, and all the subtle and rare variety of published thought and expression that exists." Book Culture particularly stands out as an essential New York literary destination and its honorable mission is best encapsulated in their own words: "As New Yorkers, we want to do our part to make sure that our city's rich history and reputation for being home to writers, publishing houses, editors, and bookstores, remains intact—as does our city's position as the literary capital of the world."

St. Agnes Library

444 Amsterdam Avenue

St. Agnes Library is one of the branches built with money Andrew Carnegie gave to the city. It opened its doors on Amsterdam Avenue in 1906. Originally a parish library at St. Agnes Chapel in 1893, the library grew into a neighborhood one in 1894 as the community was expanding. It was only in 1901 that it consolidated with the NYPL.

Today, the St. Agnes Library is beloved by many Upper West Siders, and has been a cherished landmark for more than a century. This local library, which serves as a neighborhood staple, is spacious, airy, pleasant, and has a large staircase running through it, which gives the library a comforting scent—perhaps thanks to the polish used on its steps and banister.

St. Agnes is not just a local Upper West Side library that brings back lovely memories for many of its patrons; it was also one of the branches that used to have a custodial apartment above it, where George King Washington lived when he worked as a library custodian. To find out a little more, I spoke to Sharon Washington, his daughter and only child, who grew up in the magical St. Agnes Library as a little girl, with her parents, her grandmother, and her dog.

Sharon Washington

Actor and writer
Grew up in a custodial apartment
above St. Agnes Library

What was the most special part of living in a library?
Being able to slip down into the closed library and wander around by myself after hours. Not only roaming through the bookshelves, but also moving freely in and out of all the spaces closed to the public. Like the librarians' workroom in the back, where they repaired old volumes. It had a metal spiral staircase and I can still smell the mucilage glue they used. I also remember using the old-style book checkout charging machine that took a picture of your library card and the book you were checking out. They were huge and made a whirring sound and the lights flashed—very dramatic alone at night. All part of my nighttime library world.

Aside from constantly being surrounded by books and knowledge, what were some of the main differences you experienced with your peers at school due to living in a library?
I was a very advanced reader. A combination of living in the library and reading a lot on my own, and reading not just children's books but stuff that was much more advanced that I'd find when I roamed around in the Adult section of the library after hours. I was fascinated by a lot of the science books with illustrations. So my vocabulary and science aptitude had a head start.

You performed and wrote many stories, and most recently the play **Feeding the Dragon,** *about your very unique experience living in a library as a kid. What impact did living in a library have on you?*
I'm an only child of older parents, who both worked full-time jobs, so I had a lot of alone time. But I never really felt alone. To this day I still like my solitude—and of course a good book! I am also a very social person. Living in the library fueled my imagination and exposed me from a very early age to the possibilities of a larger world. Other cultures, lives, and experiences. It gave me a thirst to learn and explore and I believe that's how I ended up in the creative field as a performer and storyteller. I love hearing and sharing stories. I think the more we know about each other and the world we live in, the less afraid of the "other" we'll be, and we can see how we as humans are more alike than we are different.

What were some of the ways in which living at St. Agnes inspired you to become such a great storyteller and actress?
Again, I think as an only child of older parents I was a little precocious and kind of a smarty-pants. I was around a lot of adults. I liked listening to their conversations. So I learned to be quiet and observe so I wouldn't get thrown out of the room—I took a lot in. I could also mimic people's gestures and voices—I was a big hit at my mother's parties! Then I'd go to school and entertain my friends by retelling the stories I'd heard at home (I'm sure not all of which I should've shared)—my very first "shows."

What was your favorite book as a kid to get from St. Agnes?

There was a big illustrated book of fairy tales—I don't remember the specific edition. I've searched for it over the years and I'd know it if I saw it. I can still remember some of the illustrations quite clearly. And the library also had the full set of twelve *Andrew Lang's Coloured Fairy Books*; Blue through Lilac— I read them all!

Where is the best place to read in St. Agnes?

It's changed quite a bit since I lived there and there was a major renovation in the mid-2000s. So the library I remember is greatly reconfigured. I used to love reading on a little chair in a corner of the Children's Library, which was on the third floor when I lived there. There were large windows facing a back alley. But I'm sure you can still find some great nooks and crannies. And all those great windows are still there.

What are some of the secrets we don't know about St. Agnes, or living in a library in general?

That there used to be a metal spiral staircase that linked the librarians' workroom in the back to the second floor, which was then the Reference Section. And there was a working dumbwaiter that went from the basement all the way to the top floor to transport books. I think it's still there—but of course not in use. And living in a library always involved climbing stairs. Lots and lots of stairs. All the apartments I knew of were on the top floor.

Do you still pay visits to St. Agnes? And if so, what types of books do you borrow from there?

I don't get back to St. Agnes that much anymore (although I have been back recently to partner and do promotions for *Feeding the Dragon*). I live in a different part of the city, so my local branch is the Mid-Manhattan Library, and I also frequent the Performing Arts Library at Lincoln Center. These both have amazing collections and when I borrow it's usually from these branches. Although with the advent of the internet I don't borrow as much as I used to unless I'm doing research for a project— either writing or researching a role. Then I can spend hours in the stacks!

I believe people lived in custodial apartments up until the 1990s. Do you think living in a library is something that would ever be brought back today or in the future?

I think the last custodian actually left in the 2000s. I don't think the custodial job will ever be brought back. There's no longer any need for a full-time custodian. My father's job was mostly to keep the coal furnace burning, and since that no longer exists there's nothing that requires a 24/7 presence. I'm sure it's also an insurance nightmare for the library as an institution. I never thought about it before, but to allow "strangers"—which would be anyone we as the live-in family would have over for dinner or a party or whatever, with the possibility of the guests being able to roam freely once the library was closed—well, these days I'm sure just seems crazy. It's a different time. But back then . . . it was magical.

Bank Street Bookstore
2780 Broadway

As we all know by now, my favorite kind of bookshop is a children's bookshop. Not just because I love kids and the books they read, but also because I prefer the way those books look and the amount of color there usually is in a kids' bookstore. I must also confess that there are probably more kids' books that I have read and cherished than adult books—but let's not get into that.

The Upper West Side had the perfect bookshop for me with its famed Bank Street Bookstore, which relocated to its current location a few years ago. On the corner of Broadway and 107th Street, and with its big orange awning, colorful is exactly what this legendary bookshop is. Mostly catering to children, parents, and teachers, the selection at Bank Street Bookstore is very well curated and nicely arranged within the cute shelves of the store. Whether you have your own kids who need books, other kids you need to gift books to, or, like me, you are a kids' book enthusiast even as an adult, Bank Street Bookstore is a must. They also host readings and author events on a regular basis.

HARLEM & WASHINGTON HEIGHTS

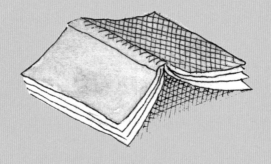

Starting north of Central Park and stretching up to 155th Street, you will find arguably the most culturally historic neighborhood in all of New York, and perhaps the modern western world: Harlem. These brownstone-flanked blocks have long been home to artists, writers, musicians, and intellectuals. Harlem residents are responsible for some of the past century's most important contributions to American culture and have left an indelible mark on modern society.

During the Harlem Renaissance of the 1920s, just a few of the neighborhood's countless notable residents included Zora Neale Hurston, Duke Ellington, Countee Cullen, W. E. B. Du Bois, James Weldon Johnson, Marcus Garvey, James Baldwin, and Ralph Ellison. In recent years, Harlem, like much of New York, has undergone dramatic demographic and socioeconomic change. Many of the legendary jazz clubs have disappeared, Columbia University continues to muscle its way into the neighborhood, and tourists take a north-bound pilgrimage to snap selfies in front of the Apollo's iconic marquee.

But from the Hudson River to the Harlem River, Uptown's blocks remain home to scores of beautiful old churches, local shops, and vibrant cultural institutions, like the Langston Hughes townhouse on East 127th Street, the Countee Cullen New York Public Library (which used to be the home of A'Lelia Walker), the Schomburg Center for Research in Black Culture, the National Black Theatre, and, of course, some of the most interesting bookshops in the city, from Revolution Books on Malcolm X Boulevard to Sister's Uptown Bookstore and Word Up Community Bookshop over in Washington Heights.

Revolution Books
437 Malcolm X Boulevard

Walking down Malcolm X Boulevard, it is hard to miss Revolution Books. Its big front window is plastered with Marxist slogans, flyers for upcoming rallies and readings, and provocative, hilarious political cartoons. Once inside, it is abundantly clear that yes, Revolution Books is all about revolution!

Founded to support the new-Marxist ideology and teachings of Bob Avakian, the chairman of the Revolutionary Communist Party, the collective is one-part buzzing political headquarters and one-part bookshop, with the shelves lined with everything from James Baldwin and Ta-Nehisi Coates to Esi Edugyan's latest work of fiction. The shop's staff is incredibly helpful, offering both literary recommendations as well as quick takes on the fascist military-industrial complex that is ruining the world. Even the most boring, selfish conservative would enjoy Revolution Books.

The Langston Hughes House
20 East 127th Street

Nestled among a row of townhouses on East 127th Street is Langston Hughes House, the home of one of the most important leaders of the Harlem Renaissance. The four-story brownstone served as a cultural epicenter not only for the neighborhood, but for an emergent scene. It was the resting place for Hughes and his convention-shattering poetry and prose, as well as a magnet for Harlem's intellectuals and artists of the 1950s and 1960s.

The Langston Hughes home was recently saved from an uncertain future and preserved by the award-winning author Renée Watson and her I, Too, Arts Collective. Watson and her organization are dedicated to carrying on Hughes's mission of supporting the local arts by offering workshops, panels, book readings, and more, at his home.

Today, visitors can wander the main living rooms, where Hughes entertained and debated. You can even check out Langston's grand piano, where he used to tickle the ivories for his dear friend Nina Simone and many other great artists.

Renée Watson

New York Times best-selling author, activist and educator, and I, Too Arts Collective founder

How does your work at I, Too Arts Collective and your work as an author feed each other?

I write for children. I'm also a poet and grew up reading poetry and Langston Hughes's work, and very much needed that mirror of looking into literature and seeing my reflection looking back at me.

I'm connected to his work personally as a writer. Originally, it came from my conversations with young people talking about the work of Langston Hughes and Maya Angelou and Lucille Clifton and all these poets I grew up on, and making sure we don't lose the physical space. It is one thing to think about someone you love and hold them in your heart and know that their legacy exists in the world, but to actually have a space where you can go and feel his presence and be inspired and reminded that this person was here and contributed to the world in a very profound way I think is powerful for young people and for emerging writers.

Did you always know that you wanted to be a children's and young adult author?

I knew I always wanted to be a writer, but I didn't know I could be an author and do that full-time. I grew up in Portland, Oregon, where I was raised. My family didn't have a whole lot of money, so when the holidays came I would write people poems and give them as gifts. I sometimes felt embarrassed and ashamed, but so many times people would say "Oh, your poem touched me, it made me cry, I'm going to save it and frame it and keep it forever." And I'd be like, what, my words moved you?

I learned really early that my words had power, and that I didn't have a lot of wealth but I had something that I could offer. So from a very early age I've been a writer. I knew I needed to write for my own sanity and to process the world.

What was your favorite book as a kid?

Some of my favorite books were in the Ramona series, because Ramona lived in Portland, Oregon. I recognized those streets and knew all those places she was talking about, and that was powerful for me. I really grew up reading poetry as a kid because there weren't a lot of books given to me that had African-American families in them, kids who looked like me, people who talked like the people at my church or on my block. Poetry was the first literature that I saw myself in, and I gravitated to that right away. I grew up reading Maya Angelou, Lucille Clifton, Gwendolyn Brooks, Langston Hughes, of course, and Margaret Walker. High school is when I really started reading novels and books and fell in love with Toni Morrison, Zora Neale Hurston, and Lorraine Hansberry.

Tell me the role this house played in the Harlem community?

Langston would have Nina Simone, James Baldwin, and friends come over to talk shop and talk politics. People called him the "People's Poet." He was very giving and loved to have parties and gatherings here, and he really loved young people. In the front yard he had a garden where kids from the block came and helped him plant, and he named flowers after them. This space was definitely Harlem's house, in a way.

Today, what role does I, Too Arts play in the Harlem community, especially among young people?

We really are working to be a place where young people feel validated and seen, and where they can come tell their stories. So many times adults are speaking on behalf of young people by way of statistics about their neighborhoods and a lot is on the negative things, so this is a space where people can come and put on the record who they are in their own words.

We see this hopefully as not just a safe haven, but a brave haven, a brave space where people can come and write their own poems and share their own stories. For adults in the neighborhood and local artists, it is a space where they can come and put on shows, put on readings, and congregate. We wanted to make sure this wasn't just a museum. Don't just come look, come and participate and be part of what's happening here.

How long has I, Too Arts had the space, and who had the space before?

It has only been since February 2017, so we are a baby. Langston lived here in 1967 when he passed away. He left it to a friend and that friend kept it until 1985 and then sold it to the owner who still has it. It's not that far removed from Langston. It just wasn't being used in a way for the community to come here. The current owner is very supportive of us and a believer in the vision.

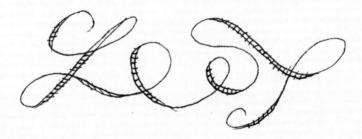

Word Up Community Bookshop
2113 Amsterdam Avenue

Sitting on the southeast corner of 165th Street and Amsterdam Avenue, Word Up Community Bookshop is what you might easily call Washington Heights's literary crown jewel. Cozy, intimate, and ever-so-friendly, Word Up is not just rows and rows of marvelous books in an unbeatable atmosphere—it is also something of a literary and cultural sanctuary for the entire neighborhood.

Word Up first debuted in summer 2011 a few blocks up the road, at 176th Street and Broadway, as a pop-up shop run by a collective of volunteers. Initially meant to be there for only a month, it actually lasted a whole year based purely on its popularity in the neighborhood. Even after losing that location due to a steep increase in the rent, the collective continued to operate by scheduling literary events and giving out books to its community.

After the collective managed to raise more than seventy thousand dollars from about eight hundred people, Word Up opened in its current location in summer 2013. The bookshop is run entirely by part-time volunteers—more than sixty people from all over New York (though most are local)—with the exception of its founder, who is there full-time.

Many of the books at Word Up are in Spanish—perhaps a third of their stock—reflecting the interests and cultures of the Washington Heights residents. A total of 85 percent of the books are secondhand, and the rest are new. Word Up also has a very large selection of comics, most of which were donated by DC Comics when they moved their headquarters from New York to Los Angeles.

Aside from selling wonderful books and being a neighborhood staple, Word Up also acts as a meeting place within its community. The store hosts many events on a weekly or biweekly basis, like their teen open mic night or their "No Name" workout show, open to people who wish to share their own comedy or stories every Tuesday—not to mention their famous storytime for kids every Saturday. When I was there late on a Friday evening, the Poetry Club was about to begin, and older men in flat caps and flannel coats were lining up while Elizabeth Acevedo, winner of the 2018 National Book Award for Young People's Literature, was finishing up her signing.

Sister's Uptown Bookstore
1942 Amsterdam Avenue

Established nearly two decades ago, this delightful bookshop is run by a charming mother and daughter duo. Warm, inviting, and homey, there is a true sense of community and openness at Sister's Uptown. During one of Sister's (more or less) weekly book signings, I met with the very friendly Kori Wilson, founder Janifer Wilson's daughter. She walked me through the shop, with its fabulous book selection (both new and secondhand titles), and presented me with the wide array of talented African American authors they are showcasing for the various events Sister's hosts. Kori and Janifer have created a real hub for members of the community in a lovely setting. The motto of Sister's is: "Knowledge of Self is the key to Understanding."

When I asked why the bookshop was called Sister's, rather than Mother and Daughter, Kori explained that the name came from the sense of creating a safe space where women could meet and bond, while discussing ideas to "nurture their minds, hearts, and souls" in a literary and cultural environment open to everybody. The shop truly reflects that idea and has a welcoming warmth to it that is unique. With its little boutique of crafts and beautiful handmade goods and art in the back of the shop, its colorful and cute kids' section to the right (Kori's four-year-old daughter was there greeting customers!), and its little, low-key café to the left, Sister's Uptown Bookstore is a one-of-a-kind gem well worth the trip.

Sigrid Nunez

Best-selling author of seven novels, winner of many literary awards including the 2018 National Book Award for Fiction, New York City native and resident

Sigrid Nunez

Tell me about your personal library, and how it reflects your own writing.
My personal library has gotten smaller over the years because I keep pruning it, wanting to keep only those books of greatest importance to me. But it happens fairly often that I end up replacing a book I'd gotten rid of. Unsurprisingly, most of my books are works of fiction or poetry.

What was your favorite book as a child?
Fairy tales of the Brothers Grimm.

When you won the National Book Award for Fiction for **The Friend,** *you spoke of the impact of growing up surrounded by people who believed the ultimate pursuit in life was reading and writing. As a dyed-in-the-wool New Yorker, can you describe a seminal moment when the community here nurtured and supported your passion and growth as a writer?*
There was no single seminal moment. What I said at the NBA ceremony was that, as a child, I was lucky enough to have had a mother and teachers who taught me that whatever happened in life, however bad things might get, I could always escape by reading a book. And I was lucky enough to keep on meeting people—dedicated teachers and dedicated writers—who believed that reading and writing were the best things a person could do with her life. Without such people I might never have become a writer.

What is your favorite place to acquire books in New York?
I have two favorites: Three Lives & Company and the Strand.

THE BRONX

The uppermost of New York's boroughs, and the county that leads up along the Hudson upstate, the Bronx has long been better known for its contributions to food, music, film, World Series rings, and street culture than for its literary connections. In fact, when Barnes & Noble closed its location here in 2016, the borough was left without a bookstore, and book-loving residents were obliged to journey down into Manhattan to satisfy any desire for books that their local libraries might not fulfill. As the poet Ogden Nash wrote in 1931: "The Bronx?/No thonx."

But there is more to the borough than might meet the bibliophile's eye. Passionate readers will know something of the place from its appearance in some of the most significant novels of recent times, including E. L. Doctorow's *Billy Bathgate* and its back-drop for pandemonium in Tom Wolfe's *Bonfire of the Vanities*. The best-selling novelist Don DeLillo grew up here and would set parts of his classic *Underworld* in his native county; much of the work of the Pulitzer Prize–winning Natalie Angier is informed by her youth here; and one of America's greatest writers, Edgar Allan Poe, called the borough home for many years. And now, with the founding of a new independent bookstore, the borough is embracing its literary heritage in the most forward-looking way. So while you may first venture to the Bronx for other reasons—to visit the magnificent zoo, or the legendary Italian delis of Arthur Avenue, or the beautiful botanical garden—it's worth seeking out some literary landmarks while you're there, too.

The Lit. Bar
131 Alexander Avenue

After the closure of the Bronx's Barnes & Noble location in 2016, Bronx resident Nöelle Santos decided that a borough of almost one-and-a-half million people without a bookshop simply would not do. So, through a mixture of passion, crowd-funding, and community outreach, she founded the wonderful Lit. Bar. Part bookstore, part wine bar, and part community events space, the Lit. Bar is an oasis for all things literary, with a fresh selection of fiction and nonfiction, and an especially good stock of poetry—much of which is by local authors and reflects the colorful and multicultural demographic of the borough. In fact, according to Santos, part of the Lit. Bar's mission is to "bring the Bronx inside"—and to create an environment that feels like the product of the community, from the graffiti on the walls outside to the voices contained in the books on the shelves.

New York Botanical Garden Shop
2900 Southern Boulevard

While there are botanical gardens and parks in each of the city's other boroughs, the New York Botanical Garden in the Bronx is the largest and most beautiful of them all. A National Historic Landmark, with 250 acres ranging from wild rambles and woods to manicured gardens and conservatories, the garden is one of the city's great treasures and well worth a visit in its own right. But less well known is the fact that the Botanical Garden is also a highly respected publisher of landscape and gardening books, and that its shop has one of the best selections of horticultural books in the world. As well as editions produced by the NYBG itself, the shop carries everything from handy guides to home gardening and academic volumes on plant science, and stunning coffee-table books of landscape and garden photography. They even sell a carefully chosen selection of cookbooks, all based on incorporating vegetables, herbs, spices, and other greenery in your cooking. It's the perfect spot for anyone with an interest in horticulture, and a great place to find pages for your green-thumbed loved ones to flick through.

Edgar Allan Poe Cottage
2640 Grand Concourse

Fittingly for a writer whose style remains utterly unique in the American canon, the Edgar Allan Poe Cottage stands out in the Bronx like a sore thumb. Set within Poe Park, which is what remains of some grassy farmland alongside Grand Concourse—a major urban thoroughfare that was originally designed to be New York's answer to Paris's Champs-Elysées—this humble cottage was Poe's home for the latter years of his life in the mid-nineteenth century. Although the great mystery writer is often associated with Manhattan, where he spent many years working as a journalist in TriBeCa and living in Greenwich Village and other areas downtown, Poe wrote many of his best-loved poetry here and some of his finest short stories, including "The Cask of Amontillado." The cottage has been operated as a historic house museum by the Bronx County Historical Society since 1975, and is open for visitors Thursdays through Sundays year-round. Some of Poe's books are preserved there, along with the desk he wrote at and the bed he slept in, and the mood of the house is so spartan and peaceful that it only magnifies your appreciation for the imagination responsible for all those intricate and magnificently grotesque stories.

Richard Price

Best-selling author of many novels,
screenwriter for television shows,
Harlem resident, Bronx native

Richard Price

*What types of books are in your book collection? I
expect most people would think you have lots of New
York books, or books about crime or cities and the
urban experience—what is the most unexpected book
in there?*

My books are so varied. I don't know what would be considered eclectic. I don't consider myself a crime writer, so it's not
like I have a great crime library. It's just everything. I guess the
most interesting thing I have is nineteenth-century sociological studies of poverty in New York
City. I have a pretty big collection of that. I've read all of it. These are obscure people. Some of it
is obvious writers, like Jacob Riis, but most of these people, I can't even tell you who they are . . .
Just somebody from that time, who was doing that type of writing and research.

In your opinion, what is the most "New York" area in Manhattan to set a novel?

The thing about New York is there is no "central" New York. Every community has its own
personality, and it's all equally "New York" . . . When you talk about New York movies, do you
talk about Woody Allen, Spike Lee, or are you talking about Whit Stillman, Martin Scorsese…?
There's a million New Yorks, not one of them is more or less important than any other. There is
not one New York quintessential area.

*I know you do a lot of research on the ground for your writing. Talk to me about that
process, and some of the most interesting experiences you have had.*

Well, this is where I was born, this is where I live, and probably this is where I'll die. I'm from
New York and I've been here all my life. In terms of going out on the street and hanging out with
people, depending on what you are working on, certain people are more important than others,
depending on the subject and the scene that I am looking at. I used to do ride-alongs with police,
and if I need to know what it's like to be a judge, I'll talk to a judge. If I need to know what it's
like to be an ice-cream man, I'll hang out with an ice-cream man. It can be anybody and everybody. I guess I'm most known for "policier"–type things, but it's only because I was writing that
type of stuff that I needed that information. It's different for every book.

Tell me about the New York literary scene?

There is no New York literary scene. Everybody thinks there's a literary scene, that all these writers hang out at one or two bars, or all the literatis go out to Brooklyn and buy brownstones. I've never been part of a literary scene. I mean, I'm sure the writers who know each other, they hang out. But it's not like a physical thing. I do remember back in the 1970s, there would be a few bars that were known for their collection of writers, like this one place in the village called the Lion's Head, which was haunted primarily by journalists and novelists of the male persuasion. But that's gone. Writing is an isolated thing. If you go to a dinner and there are three other writers there, I guess you can say that's the literary scene. But I don't know, I've never been part of one. You just hang out with your friends, and if your friends happen to do what you do, you know? Is there a plumber scene? It's the same thing. It's just a job.

What was your favorite book as a kid?

Depends what age. But there was a series of books—I guess they would be considered young adult books, but they weren't defined like that particularly—I started reading them in fifth grade. There was a series of them, maybe Random House published them. They were called the Landmark Books Series, and they weren't fiction, they were historical and biographical and they involved world history and American history. That is what I remember reading, maybe one a week for years.

I read that you prefer to write books over television. Is that still the case?

I prefer to write books, but I will starve. I like writing television if I'm writing for certain people—if I'm not writing for networks, for example. The smaller the audience, the better it is for me, because the less they need to appeal to the maximal number of people—so the less you can be individualistic when you write for a network, because you are writing for the entire country with all its taste or lack thereof. But if I am writing for premium cable like HBO, I'm going to have more freedom to write what I want, because there are no commercials, so I don't have to appeal to the buyers of cars or insurance or anything. I don't have to write in buyers' cliffhangers to prevent people from changing channels.

Is the process of writing books and TV very different?

Sure. TV is writing for the screen, it is two-dimensional—people say things and do things. Writing novels, you get into the inner life, there is actual real writing involved. There is no real writing involved in TV, there is no prose in TV writing or movie writing. It is just basically stage directions and dialogue. So it is the whole difference in the world.

A very common thing to say is that TV is the new novel. And that's crap, because it is not. For TV, you depend on actors, on the networks, on directors, on editing rooms—it's theatrical, whereas novels are words on a page. The only reason people say TV is the new novel is because it is now more episodic, and you have to spend more time to develop a character, and you have more time to stretch out a story, so it is like Dickens publishing his novel in installments in a magazine. But that's it. Everything else is two-dimensional and four-dimensional.

BROOKLYN

Culturally, Brooklyn plays an essential role within New York's literary scene. Kings County's literary pedigree is as remarkable and varied as the borough itself, and ranges from historic libraries to brand new bookstores owned by contemporary novelists. It in fact could warrant its very own booklover's guide! The very landscape of the place is replete with symbols of its literary past, both as setting for some of the most celebrated novels of the twentieth century and as home and muse to some of America's greatest writers. William Styron wrote *Sophie's Choice* here; Michael Chabon's Kavalier and Clay had all sorts of amazing adventures here; Paul Auster's follies were here; Betty Smith's tree grew here, in Williamsburg; and Jonathan Lethem built his Fortress of Solitude in Boerum Hill. The railings along the waterfront of Brooklyn Bridge Park are even inscribed with lines from longtime resident Walt Whitman's poem, "Crossing Brooklyn Ferry."

With such a storied history, it should come as no surprise that Brooklyn is still home to a lively and engaging literary world, and to some of the city's finest bookstores. While Brooklyn itself is roughly twice the size of Manhattan, a great many of the borough's most historically important literary destinations are concentrated along what you might call the Brooklyn Riviera, the string of older and more commercial neighborhoods closest to the East River that divides Long Island from Manhattan. So explore the historic houses of Brooklyn Heights (where Truman Capote and Norman Mailer wrote their masterpieces); roam the hipster haunts of Williamsburg and Bushwick, where independent bookstores perfectly reflect their communities; hear poetry in Prospect Heights or visit the borough's largest library at Grand Army Plaza; and shop for novels written by your neighbors in Park Slope and Carroll Gardens.

The Center for Fiction
15 Lafayette Avenue

You may have heard about the Mercantile Library—which was what The Center for Fiction first started as at 49 Fulton Street, on February 12, 1821. Or you may also have stumbled upon the institution's erstwhile and ever-so-charismatic 47th Street location (the former home of the novelist F. Hopkinson Smith) on a random stroll through Midtown. After nearly two centuries in Manhattan, the famed and beloved Center—the only nonprofit in America devoted solely to the art of fiction—relocated to an eighteen thousand square-foot location in Downtown Brooklyn in early 2019, joining culturally significant neighbors such as the Brooklyn Academy of Music and the Mark Morris Dance Group. The Center has a vast library and reading rooms, and will expand its revered program of discussions and events (for literature lovers of all ages) in its state-of-the-art auditorium. Readers can also visit its huge new bookshop—and pick up a coffee or a glass of wine from the café to sip while you read.

Truman Capote's House
70 Willow Street

Down by the East River, in the charming and historic Brooklyn Heights, Truman Capote lived in the basement apartment of the nineteenth-century townhouse at 70 Willow Street. The house at the time was painted yellow, but has since been restored to red brick. He is known to have written parts of *Breakfast at Tiffany's* and *In Cold Blood* there. He had deep affection for the neighborhood, and wrote *A House on the Heights* about the neighborhood's "splendid contradictions," as well as *Brooklyn Heights: A Personal Memoir,* which was originally published in one of my favorite magazines, *Holiday*. While the house itself is a private residence and not open to the public, most of the neighborhood remains unchanged from the place Capote described so well, and to walk around the beautiful streets nearby only makes his writing more visceral.

Powerhouse Arena
28 Adams Street

Not far north along the Promenade from Brooklyn Heights, in Dumbo, is the relatively new home of Powerhouse, a lovely bookstore affiliated with the publisher of the same name. Powerhouse's Arena was, until its closing in 2016—when the shop moved to its current location—one of the iconic cultural venues of the borough, with a vast space that hosted events from book signings to art exhibitions and DJ'd parties. The bookstore is smaller now, but still reflects the Powerhouse identity, with a nicely curated mix of contemporary fiction, New York–centric nonfiction, and illustrated books on art, design, and Powerhouse's specialty, photography. The space hosts literary events in its Gatherings Under the Arch series—a nod to its location beneath the archways of the Manhattan Bridge—and also stocks a nice selection of gifts, from greeting cards to prints and mugs, many with a literary twist. And just a few blocks away, by Walt Whitman's ferry landing, you could get a bite at the renowned River Café—where Bret Easton Ellis's Patrick Bateman used to go for dinner, before killing a victim or two. Something of a Brooklyn institution since opening in 1977, the restaurant is referenced in a few literary works and is a fine spot for a meal after a day of literary exploring.

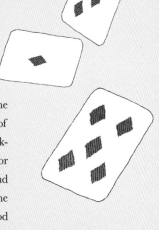

Books Are Magic
225 Smith Street

In Cobble Hill, you could spend a while browsing through Books Are Magic, the delightful shop opened in 2017 by the novelist Emma Straub, best-selling author of *Modern Lovers* and *The Vacationers*. Having opened not long after the sad demise of Book-Court—the long-standing bookstore on nearby Court Street that was a local favorite for decades—Books Are Magic was immediately adopted as a hub by residents of (and visitors to) this very culture-forward neighborhood. Under Straub's careful eye, the store's selection is surprisingly broad and brilliantly curated, with a particularly good range of contemporary fiction and poetry. And with its owner's chops, the shop has quickly become an epicenter for book launches and signings by the hottest writers of the moment, many of whom would rather have an event here than at some larger and less characterful stores in Manhattan. The store is also filled with surprising treasures and fun activities—such as "hidey-holes" for children and gumballs filled with poetry—and personalized copies of Emma Straub's own books are always available, upon request.

Community Bookstore
143 Seventh Avenue

Between the Gowanus Canal and Prospect Park, in the highly desirable area of Park Slope, the Community Bookstore has been a good neighborhood staple since 1971. In spite of the looming presence of the large branch of Barnes & Noble, which stands just ten blocks up Seventh Avenue, Community has endured with a charm and independence all its own. The shelves are stocked with a reliable selection of classics, new fiction, and nonfiction, and their "staff picks" are usually farther from the beaten path than those at less adventurous stores. There's a small garden out back, where you can pause to read or take a breather from the busy shop floor. And the best parts of the shop may be its animal hosts—Tiny the cat, and a turtle—who are minor celebrities of the neighborhood. Community Bookstore also has a sister bookshop, called Terrace Books, which opened in 2013 a little further south in Windsor Terrace.

The Central Library
10 Grand Army Plaza

Around Prospect Park, the literary world becomes your oyster: an array of all sorts of book-related destinations surround the park, and none of them are disappointing in the slightest. The first and most obvious is the Brooklyn Public Library, or more specifically the Central Library branch of the Brooklyn Public Library, which of course has a whole system of its own—the public libraries in Brooklyn are not part of the NYPL. This particular branch is indeed difficult to miss, with its breathtaking and impressive façade visible and unsurpassable from any angle of Grand Army Plaza. In fact, its design supposedly represents an open book: the spine is on the Plaza, while Eastern Parkway and Flatbush Avenue are home to the two wings opening like pages. Though the Brooklyn Park Commission chose the library's location all the way back in 1889, it was not until February 1941 that its doors opened to the public. Today, a total of about 1.7 million volumes are in circulation throughout the library, and 1.3 million people visit the place on a yearly basis—with a lovely lobby of cafés and pie shops a pleasant reward for their studiousness. Situated near the library, another noteworthy literary pit stop around the park is the Brooklyn Museum. Not only is it a great museum to visit, but its shop is worth a trip of its own. Filled with exhibition catalogues and interesting design and art books, it also has a nice selection of books about Brooklyn and New York. And adjacent to the museum, you might happily stumble into the beloved Brooklyn Botanic Garden, a one-of-a-kind natural and sensory attraction not to be missed. One of the garden's most well-kept secrets, however, is the Brooklyn Botanic Garden Library—a most adorable library filled with approximately fifteen hundred volumes from the fifteenth through the twentieth centuries of early European herbals, color-plate books, and New World floras, among other treasures. There is even a Rare Book Room for researchers in need of specialized information, containing items that are, like some of the species in the gardens themselves, either "extremely rare or irreplaceable."

Unnameable Books
600 Vanderbilt Avenue

Head north from the library and you will uncover another little gem—Unnameable Books in Prospect Heights. The store carries used books alongside new ones, but tends only to buy secondhand books in such good condition that you often can't tell which are which. The staff here also has a strong connection to poetry; several bookcases are devoted to a healthy selection of new and used collections, and readings for poets are held in the garden outside during the warmer months. And the best part of Unnameable may be its opening hours—the store almost always stays open until 11 p.m., which makes it a lovely place for night owls or bohemian locals to go browse after dinner or drinks in one of the many cool spots nearby.

Greenlight Bookstore
686 Fulton Street

A little farther north from Prospect Heights, in the Fort Greene and Clinton Hill neighborhood, you will find Greenlight Bookstore. A neighborhood favorite, this classic independent bookshop stocks titles of all genres and regularly hosts events for locals, such as book group gatherings, story time, and other original services like the first editions club, which offers one collectible new book each month to whomever subscribes. Greenlight has another branch all the way to the southeastern side of Prospect Park; but the Fort Greene branch is the mini-chain's flagship, with a constantly rotating selection in the front of the store of new literary fiction titles and a famously good section of travel books. At the other side of Fort Greene Park from Greenlight, Patti Smith and Robert Mapplethorpe used to live at 160 Hall Street. The couple used to rent the second floor of this beautiful townhouse for just eighty dollars a month, as Smith documented in her best-selling memoir *Just Kids*. I have actually been fortunate enough to spend some nice Christmassy afternoons there, as a dear friend now lives in the very same house; and despite its looking very different to the way it used to, there is still something poetic and magical about the place.

Spoonbill & Sugartown
218 Bedford Avenue

Head north from Fort Greene and you will discover Spoonbill & Sugartown—which more than justifies braving the hipsters and tourists for the trip to Williamsburg. For more than twenty years—with the exception of the newly installed branch of McNally Jackson (see page 34)—Spoonbill has been the single great bookstore in this rather trendy Brooklyn neighborhood. They sell all varieties of rare and secondhand books, as well as new material on contemporary art, literature, philosophy, and design, and carry a fabulous selection of magazines, from major art publications to independent locally published zines. They have another, smaller branch a bit further out in Bushwick—and if you do venture out east, make sure to pay a visit to Molasses Books while you're there. They offer a perfect mix of used and new books, host readings for local authors, and have a café at which customers are invited to suggest or even contribute music for everyone to listen to while they sip and browse. (On the way there, look out for a cute little used bookshop whose name alone I really like: Better Read than Dead.)

Word
126 Franklin Street

Last but not least, all the way north in Greenpoint—whose
Newton Creek divides the neighborhood from Queens—
Word is a brilliant local bookshop and a reliable resource for
consumers of new fiction and nonfiction. The store is small, so
while thoughtfully curated the selection is limited to the bigger
hits in any genre—and their signings and book club events are
rather a tight squeeze. Perhaps unique on the city's bookstore
scene, Word also hosts a summer basketball league of its own!
Apparently there is one catch, though: the league is for booklovers only. But if you are reading this book, I suppose it would
be acceptable to join.

Tavi Gevinson

Writer extraordinaire, founder of
Rookie, idol of so many young authors
and readers, and people in general,
and Brooklyn resident

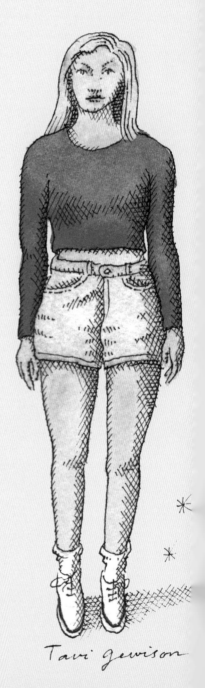

Tell me about Rookie, *and how you took it from something
you started as a child at your parents' house to the popular
destination it became.*

I started a fashion blog, *Style Rookie*, when I was eleven, and
through that community met lots of other young people who
were interested not only in fashion, but art, music, movies, and
feminism. Once I started high school, I wanted a teen magazine
that was honest, smart, creative, and had actual teens writing for
it—like the other artists and writers I had met through blogging,
and readers of my blog. I wrote on my blog that I was taking
submissions for this new online magazine I wanted to start, and
got about three thousand emails to my inbox. Among them were
people who worked in media and publishing, who helped me
learn about building the site, ad sales, finding a design studio, and
everything else that was totally foreign to me. *Rookie* launched
when I was fifteen. Its first four years were commemorated in
a print series called the *Rookie Yearbooks*, and our fifth book was
an anthology of new work by *Rookie* contributors, called *Rookie
On Love*. I'm glad that so many young people saw it as a kind of
refuge, home, and personal cheerleader.

*Seeing as you've been doing it practically since birth, what
are some of the greatest pleasures you get from writing?*

It doesn't happen all the time, but I like when the crux of what
I'm trying to say, or a connection that I've been struggling to
make, finally reveals itself, and I feel like I'm existing outside of
time and all I have to do in that moment is keep following the
train of thought and even let myself be surprised by it. That
happens probably 2 percent of the time. The rest of it I am just
recording things I already know, hoping it eventually gets me
somewhere new.

You have spent a lot of time editing teenagers' writing. Have you noticed a big change in trends of writing style in the new generation of teens compared to when you started writing?

I only feel closely attuned to *Rookie*'s corner of this generation, but I guess that is a reasonably sized chunk of this generation that is regularly writing and self-publishing.

I think that around the time *Rookie* started, the internet saw the personal essay come and go as a form of sensationalism, sometimes exploitation. Then social media mutated and knowing about people's lives and crazy stuff that happened to them became even less of a novelty.

Regardless of internet trends, young people are writing for the first time every day, and it's natural to start with yourself, your day, your diary. The writing I've seen in the *Rookie* community—from *Rookie*'s writers as well as readers—pulls from specific personal experience but is concerned with universal questions. As Elena Ferrante said, "It's only by reflecting on myself with attention and care that I can reflect on the world." I don't know if that's specific to *Rookie* or even this generation, or if it is exactly a response to social media, short-form content, outrage-mongering content, and listicles. I do think the world that people my age and teenagers are inheriting encourages self-consciousness but not really self-reflection. I think many young people are self-reflective anyway. Also: a lot of them are writing poetry! You'd think it would seem too stuffy or niche or elitist (it did for me, at first), but if you think of songwriting or lyrics and poetry as similar, poetry is actually really ubiquitous. Also, it doesn't demand that you tell your whole life story or give a researched opinion on something. It invites specificity and personal experience, which, again, is where I think most first-time writers start.

What is the best thing you've discovered about this new generation of writers?

The above!

What is the best advice you have for a young woman wanting to become an author?

Write and read as often as you can. Especially write. Don't put it off or think it's precious or spend months talking about something you want to work on—do it. (This is advice for myself.)

In your opinion, what is a must read for any young writer starting?

Something that makes you excited to write yourself. I've read lots of great books that make me love reading, but there's nothing like a book that makes you want to write, that uncovers possibilities and lets you know, yes, you can actually try that weird story/voice/structure/etc., that you've been too intimidated to try. I think Vivian Gornick's *The Situation and the Story: The Art of Personal Narrative* is a fun read, makes you want to write, and also tells you what you need to know to give that writing purpose. If I were a teacher, I'd teach it.

You started writing and working so young. Who are some of your original literary heroes?

Pippi Longstocking, Harriet the Spy, Sheila the Great, Ramona Quimby. I reread Ellen Raskin's *The Westing Game* and E.L. Konigsburg's *The View from Saturday* a lot. The main character in *The Westing Game* was my first encounter with a shapeshifter, with the idea of rebirth. *The View from Saturday* is kind of like a Glass family story about smart elementary schoolers who create their own matrix of success. If I remember correctly. In middle school I loved Sharon Creech, Sherman Alexie, Daniel Clowes, and the Sammy Keyes series.

You know teenagers better than anybody, but rumors are that they are reading less and less. What is your opinion on this, and what would you say is responsible for that shift? What can we do to make sure reading doesn't become extinct?

The world moves very fast and I must say that, by now, a teenager would know teenagers better than I do. But if these rumors are true, at least in the United States, I have some ideas:

1. Education is underfunded.

2. The humanities are undervalued.

3. American ideals are result-driven, not process-driven. If you're taught to read in order to pass a test or class, in order to eventually get into a college and then a job that promises social and financial status or, more crucially, security/survival, it's understandable that you might not consider reading for pleasure, or to learn things you won't be tested on.

4. Most people in America are just trying to make enough money to live and may not have time to read books, or to raise their kids to read books. The way TV used to be thought of as a babysitter, media/our phones equals that now. I read when I was a little kid, but I also watched a lot of TV. Like, hours a day. If I was a kid now, I would definitely want to be on my phone all the time, and if my dad wasn't literally an English teacher, I don't know how much I would have read as a kid, and therefore now, because it starts when you're young. I think the most talked-about problems with digital media, social media, and new technology—for all of their virtues—are pretty obviously the-opposite-of-reading-anything-long. Life is horrible and painful and hard, so most of the time people (including me) just want to do things that are easy. Tech companies are gaining power more rapidly and in more epic proportions than they know what to do with, and their goals tend to be meeting projections and keeping their investors happy. They're not sitting around a conference table wondering how they can help people tolerate discomfort, complexity, nuance, existential lack, the challenges of sharing a planet with other human beings—the things literature tries to engage with. Not that that's their job, though you wish everyone with massive amounts of power and influence thought about things like that. But! Living in America teaches you to have a public self (who you are at work) and a private self (your politics and beliefs), and that it's somehow respectful to keep them separate so people with power/influence are afraid of seeing how much their "private selves" actually affect decisions that their "public selves" make, and then affect the world. Anyway: I am not an economist, but I don't think it's outlandish to say that income inequality and not reading are related.

5. You asked about books, not novels, but I want to say this too: By using the language of fiction, those responsible for framing the world around us have made it into a compelling story. How could actual fiction

ever compete with the reality show that our world has become? How could novels and movies compete with the thrill of thinking you're getting someone's "real" life on Instagram, or with Trump's tweets? What character from a normal boring human being's brain could be as captivating as a real, famous rich person?

And yet, people are reading books anyway. Media is struggling, but publishing is actually doing okay. Books and niche print publications with dedicated audiences are even doing well. So to make sure reading doesn't go extinct, support independent bookstores and literary institutions that you like. Volunteer at a literacy organization and/or support politicians who care about early education.

People still want books, maybe because getting the interiority of another human being (character and/or author) is like the opposite of everything I just described, and many people are not idiots and know when they're being brainwashed and will seek out things that make them feel less like cogs. A good book makes you feel like less of a cog.

Tell me about your personal book collection. Is your work as a writer reflected in it? Do you have a most treasured book?
It's half in storage and a fourth at my parents'. I treasure many books, and reference many in my writing . . . In the last year, some of my editor's letters for *Rookie* used passages from an H. P. Lovecraft story, Ta-Nehisi Coates's last book, Mark Greif's *Against Everything*, Jacqueline Woodson's *Brown Girl Dreaming*, Tony Kushner's *Thinking About the Longstanding Problems of Virtue and Happiness* . . . I try to read a lot and then share the connections I notice across different works, periods of time, genres. I really treasure a little book called *Essays on Dolls*, with three essays by Rainer Maria Rilke, Charles Baudelaire, and Heinrich von Kleist.

What is your favorite place to get books in New York?
I would feel guilty naming one and not others. But it would be true to say museum gift shops. Maybe because the selection is smaller, so the experience is a little more pleasurable and a little less rumbling with existential dread at not having enough time to read everything.

The best place to read or write in New York?
I am constantly amazed that the library at Bryant Park isn't more full, as a place to do work. I like a park—who doesn't! And a long subway ride will do it, too. I mostly read in bed, though.

What would be the best or the worst extravagant color to paint your bookshelves?
I think all of mine are wood. Wood's nice.

QUEENS

In spite of the fact that most of New York City's visitors arrive through its John F. Kennedy and LaGuardia airports, the borough of Queens remains more the preserve of locals than tourists. Home to the Mets, a wealth of international cuisines, and some of the city's most important landmarks—from the site of the 1964 World's Fair to the Arthur Ashe Stadium and the home of the US Open—Queens is also a borough of great cultural heritage. While it might not match Manhattan or Brooklyn for literary heroes, Queens was the home of Dale Carnegie, Mitch Albom, and Toni Morrison, among others, and perhaps most famously was the setting for Michael Thomas's much celebrated novel *We Are Not Ourselves*.

Unlike the experience of exploring in its neighboring counties, whose neighborhoods are more densely packed and closer together, the booklover venturing into Queens must be prepared to travel farther afield to find the borough's best bookshops. Yet the adventures are worthwhile, not just for the stores themselves, but also for the sights along the way—from the art and industry of Long Island City to the quaint community and Tudor architecture of Kew Gardens.

The Astoria Bookshop
31-29 31st Street

The only independent bookstore in this upper corner of Queens, and a staple in the neighborhood since its opening in 2013, the Astoria Bookshop has a concise but excellent selection, offering a variety of contemporary fiction and nonfiction (and biographies in particular) in a quiet and friendly atmosphere. With solid travel and children's sections, too, and frequently changing curated displays that reflect the charm and character of the staff, the store has something of the feel of a smaller McNally Jackson to it (see page 34). The events at the store—from book signings to readings and panel discussions—draw interesting authors but also focus as often as possible on local writers, which inspires a loyal following and gives the store a truly independent feel.

Book Culture
26-09 Jackson Avenue

Book Culture—the local mini-chain whose other locations speckle the landscape of the Upper West Side (see page 169)—is an important presence in Long Island City, a neighborhood in Queens which, while culturally significant, had been lacking a good source for new books before this store opened in 2017. With less emphasis on scholarly books than you'll find at the Manhattan locations (which serve Columbia University and an altogether quite studious demographic), the selection here is focused more on brand-new fiction and poetry, with bigger hits of nonfiction and an expansive children's section alongside. Events at this charming shop—which is an airy, sky-lit space that sort of resembles a modern take on a barn—cater to the local demographic of artsy youth and young parents, with poetry readings by local writers and creative children's story times with themes like "Mozart for Munchkins." As well as their solid collection of books, the shop also carries a wonderful selection of stationery—including every single kind of Moleskine notebook and journal any poet could desire.

Artbook @ PS1
22-25 Jackson Avenue

Also in Long Island City—and testament to the artistic bent of the neighborhood, which includes the Noguchi Museum and Socrates Sculpture Park—Artbook is the bookshop housed within PS1, the contemporary art outpost of the Museum of Modern Art. In line with the mission and mood of the museum itself, Artbook carries the best selection of contemporary art books and monographs anywhere in the city, with an emphasis on work by truly cutting-edge artists and independent publishers. In addition to books, Artbook also stocks a vast range of magazines and journals, most with a focus on art, design, or photography; the store was called the best magazine shop in the city by *New York Magazine*. Since 2005, MoMA PS1 also plays host to the city's yearly Art Book Fair, which is presented in collaboration with Printed Matter (see page 102). Collectors, publishers, and booksellers from around the world set up stalls throughout the museum to display everything from new publications to vintage prints. This countercultural spirit can be felt year-round at Artbook; alongside significant catalogues they stock an amazing range of independent zines and artists' books that you just won't find anywhere else in New York (or beyond).

Topos Bookstore Cafe
788 Woodward Avenue

Further into Queens—in Ridgewood, which borders the über-hipster Brooklyn neighborhood of Bushwick—Topos Bookstore Cafe offers great new and secondhand books, as well as a café where you can indulge in a brew while enjoying some of your favorite reads. Regulars can be seen trading books for credit, which they might immediately spend on a new volume and a latte at the cozy café counter. Events at the store are perfectly informal, with local writers standing to read from their pages amid the cluttered shelves. As with any store whose stock is made up in part by used books, the selection varies, but there's always a good range of classic fiction and poetry, and shelves of nonfiction with a liberal leaning. Unusually (and charmingly) for a bookshop-cum-coffee shop, Topos proudly declares itself a WiFi-free zone, imploring its customers to read or—gasp!—talk to one another instead.

Kew and Willow Books
81-63 Lefferts Boulevard

I can think of no more fitting end to a book about New York's bookstores than to celebrate a shop that so perfectly embodies the city's bookloving spirit. Kew and Willow is located in the quaint and largely residential Queens neighborhood of Kew Gardens, not far from some of the borough's best-known attractions in Flushing Meadows—the Queens Botanical Garden, the New York Hall of Science, and Frederick Law Olmsted's beautiful Forest Park. After three nearby branches of Barnes & Noble closed and much of Queens was left without a single outlet for new books, three former booksellers from the chain joined together, raised funds through Kickstarter, and founded this charming independent bookstore in 2017. Their combination of bookselling experience with neighborhood savvy makes Kew and Willow the perfect local bookshop, with a top-notch selection of new fiction and nonfiction in the front and a charming children's and young-adult section in the back. The shop hosts grown-up events—from straightforward book signings to more creative events, like a recent wine and cheese tasting with the author of a cookbook about cheese—as well as regular children's story times and puppet shows. A real fixture of a real neighborhood, and the product of a passion for reading and for bringing books to the community, Kew and Willow is as beloved and enduring a symbol of New York's literary culture as any of the historic sites, settings, stories, and storefronts that came before it.

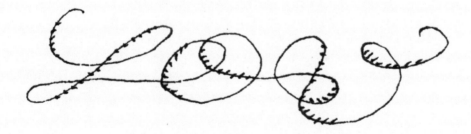

INDEX

(Page references in *italics* refer to illustrations.)

ACKNOWLEDGMENTS

One of the first people I would like to thank is my dear editor, Daniel Melamud. I appreciate him putting up with my lack of punctuality, my unkept promises, my permanent requests to add more people and places to the book, and my love of procrastination. I am also grateful for the full support and endorsement of Charles Miers and all of Rizzoli in this overambitious project.

Another person I am forever grateful to is my father, also known as Papitou, for agreeing to provide so many and such beautiful drawings. I know that the pleading and stalking was often a bit too extreme on my part. I apologize for all of it, and just cross my fingers that the result is satisfactory to him! After all, I do hope New York is the first of countless other guides to booklover cities.

Many thanks also to Geoffrey Dunne, the patient designer who put everything together at record-breaking speed and obliged all sorts of specific and last-minute demands. Jacob Lehman I believe witnessed lots of embarrassing mistakes, which have (thanks to him) since been erased.

There is an extensive list of bibliophiles (who replied to my annoying questions) that I am extremely thankful to: Otto Penzler, Joanne Hendricks, Eddie Huang, Andrew Richardson, David Strettell, Nancy Bass, Geoff Bartholomew, Hamish Bowles, Marc Jacobs, Jane Stubbs, Graydon Carter, Gary Egan, Linda Zagaria and the National Arts Club, Ed Hamilton, Max Schumann, Christopher Platt and the NYPL, Tina Brown, Harold Evans, Hervé Ferrage, Tom Freston, Nan and Gay Talese, Sharon Washington, Renée Watson, Sigrid Nunez, Richard Price, and Tavi Gevinson.

There are also the people who led me to these talented interviewees and who participated in valuable ways: Izzy Evans, who was of terrific help brainstorming and contacting people (not just her parents, but a whole cast of characters); Nicholas Vinocur my friend of nearly twenty-five years; my skilled brother-in-law Benjamin Detrick, and more.

I should definitely thank a few of my family members: my brother Alexis for dealing with every logistical aspect in Paris and any random "urgent" requests I may have summoned him with; my sister Olympia for always providing me with recommendations and ideas; and my mother for giving birth to me and also putting me in touch with some of her friends included in the book. A big thank you to the rest of my family (Tobore, Edward and Zoe especially, but also Paulette and Bambam) for everything else. Perhaps I will also mention my little son Otto, who despite being a great source of distraction, has also had wonderful insight about some of these bookish destinations. (I will not thank Alpha, his sister who was in utero during all of this—her impending arrival only slowed me down!)

Last but not least, I want to thank my husband Detrick who, aside from being a lovely husband, also ended up doubling as a very efficient, devoted, and unrewarded helper—and, of course, the greatest moral support one could ever ask for.

MY NOTES

First published in the United States of America in 2019 by
Rizzoli International Publications, Inc.
300 Park Avenue South
New York, NY 10010
www.rizzoliusa.com

Editor: Daniel Melamud
Copyeditor: Jacob Lehman
Proofreader: Tricia Levi
Design: Geoffrey Dunne
Production: Barbara Sadick

ISBN-13: 978-0-8478-6366-2
Library of Congress Control Number: 2019938581

2019 2020 2021 2022 / 10 9 8 7 6 5 4 3
Printed in Italy